Communications in Computer and Information Science

2908

Series Editors

Gang Li, *School of Information Technology, Deakin University, Burwood, VIC, Australia*

Joaquim Filipe, *Polytechnic Institute of Setúbal, Setúbal, Portugal*

Zhiwei Xu, *Chinese Academy of Sciences, Beijing, China*

Rationale

The CCIS series is devoted to the publication of proceedings of computer science conferences. Its aim is to efficiently disseminate original research results in informatics in printed and electronic form. While the focus is on publication of peer-reviewed full papers presenting mature work, inclusion of reviewed short papers reporting on work in progress is welcome, too. Besides globally relevant meetings with internationally representative program committees guaranteeing a strict peer-reviewing and paper selection process, conferences run by societies or of high regional or national relevance are also considered for publication.

Topics

The topical scope of CCIS spans the entire spectrum of informatics ranging from foundational topics in the theory of computing to information and communications science and technology and a broad variety of interdisciplinary application fields.

Information for Volume Editors and Authors

Publication in CCIS is free of charge. No royalties are paid, however, we offer registered conference participants temporary free access to the online version of the conference proceedings on SpringerLink (http://link.springer.com) by means of an http referrer from the conference website and/or a number of complimentary printed copies, as specified in the official acceptance email of the event.

CCIS proceedings can be published in time for distribution at conferences or as post-proceedings, and delivered in the form of printed books and/or electronically as USBs and/or e-content licenses for accessing proceedings at SpringerLink. Furthermore, CCIS proceedings are included in the CCIS electronic book series hosted in the SpringerLink digital library at http://link.springer.com/bookseries/7899. Conferences publishing in CCIS are allowed to use our online conference service (Meteor) for managing the whole proceedings lifecycle (from submission and reviewing to preparing for publication) free of charge.

Publication process

The language of publication is exclusively English. Authors publishing in CCIS have to sign the Springer CCIS copyright transfer form, however, they are free to use their material published in CCIS for substantially changed, more elaborate subsequent publications elsewhere. For the preparation of the camera-ready papers/files, authors have to strictly adhere to the Springer CCIS Authors' Instructions and are strongly encouraged to use the CCIS LaTeX style files or templates.

Abstracting/Indexing

CCIS is abstracted/indexed in DBLP, Google Scholar, EI-Compendex, Mathematical Reviews, SCImago, Scopus. CCIS volumes are also submitted for the inclusion in ISI Proceedings.

How to start

To start the evaluation of your proposal for inclusion in the CCIS series, please send an e-mail to ccis@springer.com

Jitendra Jonnagaddala · Hong-Jie Dai ·
Ching-Tai Chen · Yung-Chung Chang ·
Hui-Hsien Feng
Editors

Large Language Models for Automatic Deidentification of Sensitive Health Information in Clinical Speech

2025 International Workshop on Deidentification
of Electronic Medical Record Notes (2025 IW-DMRN)
Taipei, Taiwan, August 10, 2025
Revised Selected Papers

Editors
Jitendra Jonnagaddala [iD]
UNSW Sydney
Kensington, NSW, Australia

Hong-Jie Dai [iD]
NKUST
Kaohsiung City, Taiwan

Ching-Tai Chen [iD]
Asia University
Taichung City, Taiwan

Yung-Chung Chang [iD]
Taipei Medical University
Taipei City, Taiwan

Hui-Hsien Feng [iD]
NKUST
Kaohsiung City, Taiwan

ISSN 1865-0929   ISSN 1865-0937 (electronic)
Communications in Computer and Information Science
ISBN 978-981-92-2281-0   ISBN 978-981-92-2282-7 (eBook)
https://doi.org/10.1007/978-981-92-2282-7

This Springer imprint is published by the registered company Springer Nature Singapore Pte Ltd.
The registered company address is: 152 Beach Road, #21-01/04 Gateway East, Singapore 189721, Singapore

If disposing of this product, please recycle the paper.

Preface

This volume presents papers carefully selected from the 2nd International Workshop on Deidentification of Medical Record Notes (2025 IW-DMRN), which was held as part of MedInfo 2025 in Taipei, Taiwan, and organized as the concluding event of the SREDH/AI Cup 2025 Deidentification competition (https://www.sredhconsortium.org/sredh-workshops/2025-iw-dmrn). The workshop was hosted at the Taipei International Convention Centre, Taipei, Taiwan, on August 10, 2025.

The 2025 IW-DMRN was organized by the SREDH Consortium (www.sredhconsortium.org) and UNSW Sydney in collaboration with NKUST Taiwan, TMU Taiwan, and Asia University, bringing together researchers and industry partners across the Asia-Pacific region working at the intersection of privacy-preserving AI, medical natural language processing, and healthcare data governance.

The deidentification of medical record content remains a foundational requirement for enabling the safe, scalable, and ethical secondary use of healthcare data. Clinical documentation and patient-clinician communications contain highly sensitive personal information that must be protected before such data can be used for clinical research, machine learning development, healthcare analytics, and system-level quality improvement. With the rapid integration of large language models (LLMs) into healthcare workflows, the urgency of developing robust, transparent, and reproducible methods for identifying and removing sensitive health information (SHI) has increased significantly. In addition, the emergence of speech-based clinical documentation pipelines has elevated the importance of privacy-preserving approaches for medical speech and automatic speech recognition (ASR) outputs, in which deidentification must be effective despite transcription variability and linguistic diversity.

To advance progress on these challenges, we introduced the SREDH/AI Cup 2025, which was conducted between March 31, 2025, and July 16, 2025, as a community-driven initiative encouraging the development of state-of-the-art methods for privacy preservation in medical speech data. The competition consisted of two subtasks based on medical speech audio recordings. Task 1 aimed to generate audio transcriptions to support the development of speech recognition models for clinical settings. Task 2 focused on detecting SHI in the resulting transcripts. The competition was conducted using the CodaLab platform (https://www.codabench.org/competitions/4890/?secret_key=38d92718-cc4d-4907-9c65-c73419671268).

In total, 246 participants formed 149 teams. Among them, 51 teams submitted predictions, resulting in 160 valid submissions. More details on the competition are available at https://www.sredhconsortium.org/sredh-competitions/sredhai-cup-2025. Nine teams were invited to submit their manuscript, resulting in the publication of nine papers in this Springer proceedings volume. For the 2025 workshop proceedings, submissions were evaluated through a full-paper peer review process conducted in a single-blind manner. Each paper received reviews from three qualified reviewers, selected based on domain expertise in biomedical NLP, healthcare AI, and privacy-preserving computation. Papers were reviewed for scientific novelty, technical soundness, relevance to the workshop themes, clarity of presentation, and reproducibility, with additional emphasis placed on methodological transparency to ensure that the results can be validated and extended by the broader community.

We gratefully acknowledge the efforts of all authors who contributed their work to this volume and express our sincere appreciation to the scientific program committee members and external reviewers for their time, expertise, and valuable feedback throughout the reviewing process.

We acknowledge the Ministry of Education, Taiwan, for funding the competition and express our appreciation to our sponsors. We extend our gratitude to the SREDH Consortium Translational Cancer Bioinformatics working group for their support in accessing the OpenDeID corpus Dataset (https://www.sredhconsortium.org/sredh-datasets). We further thank the organizations supporting the IW-DMRN initiative, including Asus IoT Healthcare, whose contributions help strengthen research and collaboration in privacy-preserving AI for healthcare. We recognize the international community engaged through the workshop, which reflected participation across the Asia-Pacific region, North America, and Europe, and reinforced IW-DMRN as a growing forum for focused, high-impact work in this field.

This volume reflects the continued momentum in research on deidentification and privacy-preserving AI, particularly as healthcare systems increasingly adopt data-driven and generative AI technologies. We hope that the contributions in these proceedings will support future advances in protecting patient privacy, strengthening research reproducibility, and enabling responsible innovation across medical speech and electronic health record ecosystems.

April 2026

Jitendra Jonnagaddala
Hong-Jie Dai
Ching-Tai Chen
Yung-Chung Chang
Hui-Hsien Feng

Organization

General Chair

Jitendra Jonnagaddala	UNSW Sydney, Australia/ SREDH Consortium, Australia

Editorial, Organizing and Scientific Program Committee Chairs

Jitendra Jonnagaddala	UNSW Sydney, Australia/SREDH Consortium, Australia
Hong-Jie Dai	National Kaohsiung University of Science and Technology, Taiwan
Ching-Tai Chen	Asia University, Taiwan
Yung-Chun Chang	Taipei Medical University, Taiwan
Hui-Hsien Feng	National Kaohsiung University of Science and Technology, Taiwan

Scientific Program Committee

Hao-Ping Yang	National Kaohsiung University of Science and Technology, Taiwan
Hsin-Min Wang	Academia Sinica, Taiwan
Pratham Nandy	CGD Health, India
Wan-Shu Cheng	Providence University, Taiwan
Omkar Panchal	CGD Health, India
Zheng-long Wu	Soochow University, Taiwan

Keynote Speakers

Ming-Iu Lai	ASUS, Taiwan
Chao-Hsuan Ke	Innolux Corporation, Taiwan

Additional Reviewers

Divya Nadar	CGD Health, India
Hsin-Min Wang	Academia Sinica, Taiwan
Wan-Shu Cheng	Providence University, Taiwan
Zheng-Long Wu	Soochow University, Taiwan

Organizers

SREDH Consortium

Asia University, Taiwan

University of New South Wales, Australia
Taiwan

National Kaohsiung University of Science and Technology,

Sponsors

Asus IoT Healtcare

Contents

Instruction-Tuned LLMs for Multilingual Medical ASR and Privacy Entity Extraction

Jing Jin, Jui-Chien Tsou, Chih-Ho Chen, Po-Jen Ko,
and Tzu-Hung Huang

Department of Computer Science and Information Engineering, National Taiwan University,
Taipei, Taiwan
{b10204022,b11902155}@ntu.edu.tw, zionhuang1107@gmail.com

Abstract. In this study, we propose a comprehensive framework for sensitive information recognition in bilingual doctor-patient speech, developed for the AI CUP 2025 Spring Challenge. The task consists of two subtasks: automatic speech recognition (ASR) and named entity recognition (NER) for privacy-related spans. For ASR, we fine-tuned the Whisper-large-v3-turbo model separately on Chinese and English audio, achieving improved Mixed Error Rates (MER) through language-specific modeling. For NER, we reformatted the data into Alpaca-style instruction-output pairs and employed QLoRA fine-tuning on two complementary LLMs, Gemma-27B and Qwen2.5-32B-Instruct. We further applied data augmentation using semantic rewriting with a distilled Qwen-7B model and per-formed category-wise training to enhance low-frequency entity detection. To align predicted spans with timestamps, we devised a sliding window approach combined with Gemini-based LLM inference for span recovery. Finally, we integrated predictions from Gemma and Qwen using a non-overlapping span merging strategy. Our system achieved second place in the ASR subtask and ranked sixth overall, demonstrating the effectiveness of combining LLMs, instruction tuning, and hybrid post-processing for medical speech privacy protection (Our code and data for this paper are made available at: https://github.com/pango0/aicup).

Keywords: Automatic Speech Recognition · Named Entity Recognition · Medical speech privacy

1 Introduction

With the increasing use of speech-based interfaces and virtual assistants in healthcare, protecting sensitive patient information in spoken content has become a critical concern [1, 2]. Automatic de-identification of medical audio data presents several challenges, particularly in multilingual settings where language-specific patterns, transcription noise, and entity ambiguity can hinder the effectiveness of NER systems.

In this study, we address the task of detecting Sensitive Health Information (SHI) in multilingual medical dialogues, as posed in the AICUP 2025 Spring Challenge.

© The Author(s), under exclusive license to Springer Nature Singapore Pte Ltd. 2026
J. Jonnagaddala et al. (Eds.): IW-DMRN 2025, CCIS 2908, pp. 1–14, 2026.
https://doi.org/10.1007/978-981-92-2282-7_1

The competition provided audio data and corresponding SHI annotations across multiple languages, requiring participants to build an end-to-end system combining speech recognition and information extraction.

Recent evidence further underscores the importance of rigorous evaluation when applying large language models to sensitive health information de-identification. A comprehensive multi-dataset benchmarking study comparing rule-based, hybrid, and LLM-based approaches across heterogeneous electronic health record corpora [3] demonstrated that supervised fine-tuned LLMs can achieve substantially higher de-identification accuracy than traditional methods, while also revealing notable variability in performance across datasets and documentation styles. These findings highlight that corpus harmonization, cross-dataset robustness, and systematic benchmarking are essential prerequisites for the safe and reliable deployment of LLM-driven de-identification systems in real-world clinical environments [4].

Recent advances in large language models have significantly reshaped the landscape of clinical text de-identification and sensitive information extraction. However, leveraging state-of-the-art LLMs in medical privacy tasks requires rigorous benchmarking across heterogeneous datasets to ensure reliability and robustness. Prior large-scale evaluations [3] demonstrate that supervised fine-tuned LLMs consistently outperform rule-based and hybrid systems in recognizing sensitive health information, particularly under complex linguistic variations. At the same time, these studies highlight notable dataset variability, emphasizing the importance of corpus harmonization, distribution awareness and systematic comparison under realistic clinical conditions. Therefore, beyond adopting powerful instruction-tuned architectures, it is essential to benchmark models under multilingual, noisy settings to accurately assess generalization performance and practical deployment readiness in real-world healthcare environments [4, 5].

To tackle this task, we developed a two-stage pipeline combining fine-tuned ASR and instruction-based large language models (LLMs). We adopted Whisper-large-v3-turbo for ASR and fine-tuned it separately on Chinese and English datasets. For SHI extraction, we reformulated the task as a generation problem and applied QLoRA fine-tuning on two families of instruction-following LLMs: Gemma-27B and Qwen2.5-32B-Instruct.

Our main contributions are as follows:

- We constructed a bilingual ASR system by separately fine-tuning Whisper on Chinese and English speech.
- We reformulated SHI detection as an instruction-based generation task and applied QLoRA fine-tuning on Gemma and Qwen models.
- We proposed a two-step timestamp alignment strategy combining sliding window matching and LLM-based fallback to improve temporal precision.
- We ensembled multiple models via timestamp-aware merging to increase coverage and robustness.

Our approach 2-nd place in the ASR task and ranked 6-th overall in the final leaderboard, demonstrating strong robustness and generalizability in real-world medical audio scenarios.

2 Method

To address the AI CUP 2025 Spring Challenge, we developed a two-stage system that combines fine-tuned ASR with instruction-based entity recognition models. This section details the task formulation, datasets, evaluation metrics, and the design of our full pipeline.

2.1 Dataset

The study utilizes the SREDH – AI Cup SHI speech corpus 2025 which was constructed using OpenDeID v2 corpus, a clinical de-identification dataset derived from electronic medical records and adapted for multilingual doctor–patient speech processing [6]. The dataset contains Chinese and English dialogue recordings paired with transcripts and fine-grained annotations of Sensitive Health Information (SHI), including entities such as names, dates, locations, contact details, and identification numbers, each associated with temporal span information to enable alignment with audio. These characteristics make the corpus suitable for evaluating end-to-end pipelines that integrate automatic speech recognition with span-level privacy entity extraction under realistic clinical communication settings [3].

2.2 Task Formulation

The challenge comprises two subtasks:

Task 1: ASR Given an audio segment x, the goal is to transcribe it into text y:

$$f_{ASR} : x \rightarrow y$$

Task 2: Sensitive Health Information (SHI) Recognition: Given a transcript s, the goal is to extract spans of sensitive information and classify them into pre-defined categories. Each output span is associated with a label t_i and a time range $[s_i, e_i]$:

$$\{(t_i, s_i, e_i)\}_{i=1}^{N}$$

Table 1 presents the full list of fine-grained SHI labels, covering a wide range of personally identifiable information, including names, dates, locations, contact information, and identifiers.

Table 1. SHI super-categories used for class-specific training (left) and corresponding label names in the dataset (right).

SHI Category	Label Names in Data
Name	PATIENT, DOCTOR, USERNAME, FAMILYNAME, PERSONALNAME
Occupation	PROFESSION
Location	ROOM, DEPARTMENT, HOSPITAL, ORGANIZATION, STREET, CITY, DISTRICT, COUNTY, STATE, COUNTRY, ZIP, LOCATION-OTHER

(continued)

Table 1. (continued)

SHI Category	Label Names in Data
Age	AGE
Date	DATE, TIME, DURATION, SET
Contact	PHONE, FAX, EMAIL, URL, IPADDRESS
Identifiers	SOCIAL_SECURITY_NUMBER, MEDICAL_RECORD_NUMBER, HEALTH_PLAN_NUMBER, ACCOUNT_NUMBER, ID_NUMBER, LICENSE_NUMBER, VEHICLE_ID, DEVICE_ID, BIOMETRIC_ID,
Other	OTHER

2.3 Dataset and Evaluation Metrics

The dataset consists of Chinese and English doctor-patient dialogues. Training files are accompanied by transcripts and annotated SHI spans with labels and timestamps.

- **ASR Evaluation.** The task is evaluated using Mixed Error Rate (MER):

$$MER = \frac{S + D + I}{N}$$

where S, D, and I denote the number of substitutions, deletions, and insertions, and N is the number of reference tokens.

- **SHI Span Evaluation.** Entity recognition is scored by span-level macro-average F1-score. A prediction is correct if the predicted type matches and the predicted timestamp range overlaps with the ground truth. Figure 1 illustrates how span-level F1 is computed based on type match and timestamp overlap.

2.4 System Overview

We implemented a two-phase pipeline:

- **Phase1:** ASR using language-specific Whisper models.
- **Phase2:** SHI recognition using instruction-tuned LLMs with post-processing.

  Figure 2 shows an overview of our system architecture.

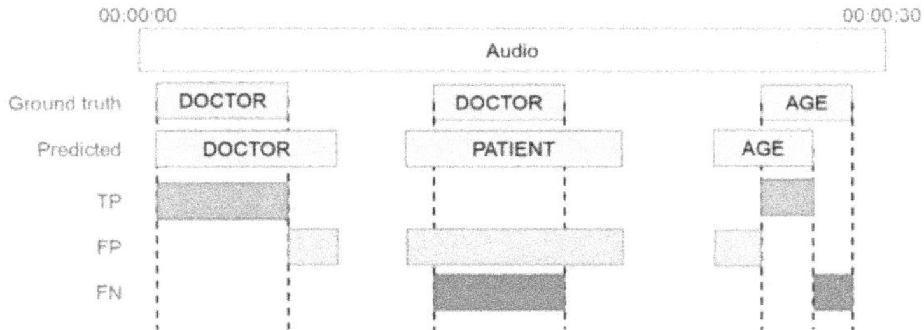

Fig. 1. Span-level F1 computation illustration. Predicted and ground truth spans must match in type and overlap in timestamp to be counted as true positives.

2.5   ASR Fine-Tuning

We used Openai/whisper-large-v3-turbo [7] as the base model for ASR. Considering the significant linguistic and acoustic differences between languages, we trained two separate models. Mandarin and English audio segments were first separated based on metadata and then processed using librosa for resampling and silence trimming.

We adopted Hugging Face's [8] Seq2SeqTrainer framework, using WhisperTokenizer and WhisperFeatureExtractor to prepare training data. Mandarin data was split 85/15 for training and validation, while the English set was split 96/4 due to its small-er size. Mandarin was trained for 5 epochs, and English for only 1 epoch to avoid overfitting. We employed a batch size of 8 per GPU and used mixed-precision (fp16) training.

Inference was performed using beam search with 5 beams. We enabled timestamp prediction via the transcribe_with_timestamps() function, which aligns each token to a segment-level timestamp. The final output included two formats:

- **Plain text transcript** (task1_(zh/en)_answer.txt):

```
Format: <id>\t<transcript>
Example: 271 No, no. That would be good for you...
```

- **Timestamped JSON** (task1_(zh/en)_answer_timestamps.json):

```
[
      {
    "text": <transcript>,
    "chunks": [
       {"text": <word>, "timestamp": [start, end]}, ...
    ],
    "num": <id>
  }, ...
]
```

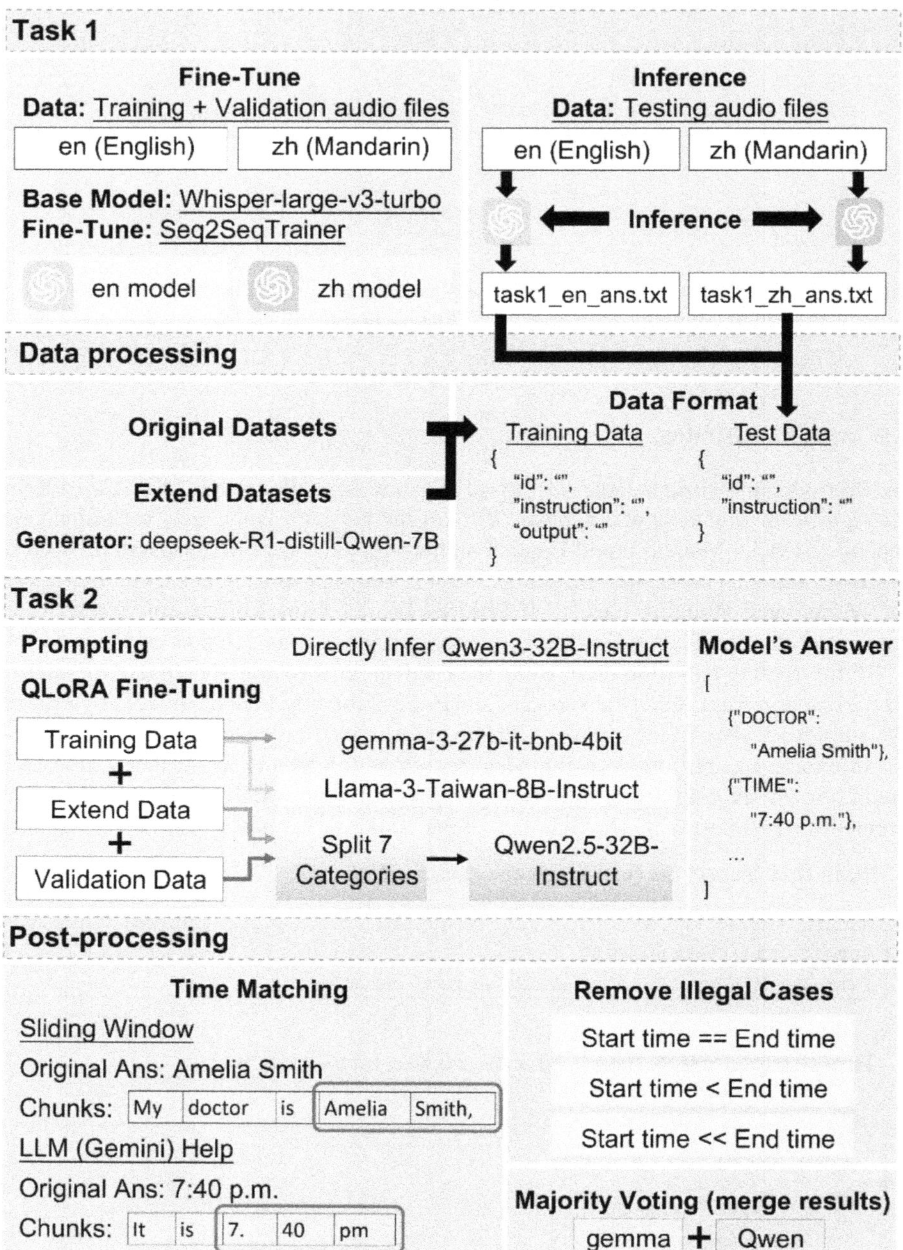

Fig. 2. Overview of our system pipeline across all stages: ASR, preprocessing, model training, and post-processing.

These outputs were then passed to the entity recognition pipeline in the next stage

2.6 Instruction-Based Entity Recognition

To convert the labeled data into a form suitable for instruction tuning, we refor-matted each sentence and its entity spans into instruction/output pairs following the Alpaca format [9]. The instruction field contains a natural-language medical sentence, and the output field is a list of extracted spans annotated with entity labels. To enrich the training set and improve the model's generalization, we extended the dataset in two ways:

- **Paraphrase augmentation:** We used deepseek-R1-distill-Qwen-7B [10] to generate semantically consistent paraphrases of the original sentences while preserving the ground-truth span labels.
- **Synthetic example generation:** For each major entity category (e.g., CONTACT, LOCATIONS), we constructed a category-specific prompt describing the labels and asked an LLM to generate realistic clinical narratives containing relevant entities. The model was instructed to return both the sentence and its corresponding labeled spans in JSON format.

In both strategies, the resulting examples were automatically validated and merged into the training set, providing a more diverse and balanced distribution of entity types.

2.7 Model Training

We adopted the QLoRA fine-tuning framework [11] to reduce memory usage and speed up training for large models. We implemented two main training configurations:

- **Gemma-3-27B (baseline) [12]:** We fine-tuned unsloth/gemma-3-27b-it-bnb-4bit using only the original training set. The model was trained with 4-bit quantization and bf16 precision, optimized via paged_adamw_32bit. While simpler, this configuration had low memory usage and fast inference, making it a strong baseline.
- **Qwen2.5-32B-Instruct [13]:** https://www.authorea.com/users/1010995/articles/137 1101-instruction-tuned-llms-for-multilingual-medical-asr-and-privacy-entity-extraction For a more powerful alternative, we combined training, validation, and augmented data and trained multiple sub models each targeting a specific subset of labels. These models were built to better generalize rare categories and support Chinese-centric recognition tasks.

All training runs used gradient checkpointing and group-by-length bucketing to save memory. Most models were trained on 4090 or H100 GPUs, using consistent hyperparameters like a learning rate of 5e-5, constant schedulers, and max steps between 100–200.

2.8 Postprocessing and Timestamp Alignment

After inference, we mapped entity spans predicted by LLMs back to the corresponding audio timestamps. Our alignment pipeline combined heuristic and model-based strategies:

1. **Sliding window matching:** We segmented the ASR transcript into overlapping windows of up to 5 chunks. For each predicted entity span, we searched the windows for exact string matches and recorded the earliest matching timestamp range. This heuristic method worked well in most cases.
2. **LLM fallback:** If no match, we fed the full sentence into Gemini-2.5-flash [14] and asked it to help identify which chunk most likely contained the span. We then used the timestamp of the containing sentence as a fallback range.

To handle ambiguity and duplicates, we filtered out spans with invalid timestamps (e.g., start $\geq$ end), and deduplicated identical spans across multiple submodels. For overlapping spans predicted by both Gemma and Qwen, we applied a priority-based merging strategy that retained only the span with the longest exact match and highest confidence.

2.9 Environment

All experiments were conducted on a Linux-based environment (Arch Linux), with Python 3.11 and PyTorch 2.2 as the primary programming and deep learning framework. We adopted the Hugging Face ecosystem for model loading, fine-tuning, and inference, using the following core libraries:

- transformers 4.50.0 — for handling pretrained models like Whisper, Gemma, and Qwen, and supporting Seq2Seq and causal decoding pipelines.
- peft 0.15.1 — for parameter-efficient fine-tuning via QLoRA, enabling large model training under memory constraints.
- bitsandbytes 0.45.5 — for 4-bit quantization, reducing GPU memory usage during fine-tuning and inference.
- datasets, evaluate — for dataset management and custom metric computation, especially in ASR and NER stages.
- librosa and torchaudio — for audio preprocessing, including silence trimming, resampling, and waveform manipulation.

Training was conducted on multi-GPU setups involving NVIDIA RTX 3090, RTX 4090, and H100 clusters, depending on model size and phase. Whisper models were fine-tuned on single-GPU nodes with FP16 precision, while large instruction-tuned LLMs (e.g., Qwen2.5-32B) were distributed across multiple H100 nodes with gradient checkpointing enabled to manage memory overhead. For prompting and fallback reranking, we used the Gemini API via the google-generativeai Python client (v0.8.5), with a context window of up to 1024 tokens. Gemini was primarily used to rerank or recover span-to-timestamp alignments when rule-based heuristics failed, providing robustness in postprocessing.

Version control and reproducibility were ensured through Git and shell-based training scripts, with seed control and logging enabled throughout all phases.

3 Experiment Results

3.1 Task 1: ASR

We fine-tuned the openai/whisper-large-v3-turbo model on Mandarin speech data provided in the AICUP 2025 challenge. The training process recorded both the training loss and validation MER (Mixed Error Rate) per epoch to observe model convergence.

As shown in Fig. 3, the training loss decreases rapidly during the first few epochs, while the validation MER begins to rebound after around 0.6–1 epoch. This indicates early signs of overfitting. To avoid this issue, we selected the checkpoint with the lowest validation MER as the final output model.

Table 2. Validation MER comparison before and after fine-tuning.

Model Setting	Valid MER
whisper-large-v3-turbo (base)	0.0996
Fine-tuned model	**0.0813**

As shown in Table 2, the fine-tuned model achieved a significantly lower MER on the validation set. This indicates the effectiveness of our training strategy. On the official Codabench leaderboard, our final submission for Task 1 ranked second place overall, demonstrating the robustness and competitiveness of our ASR pipeline.

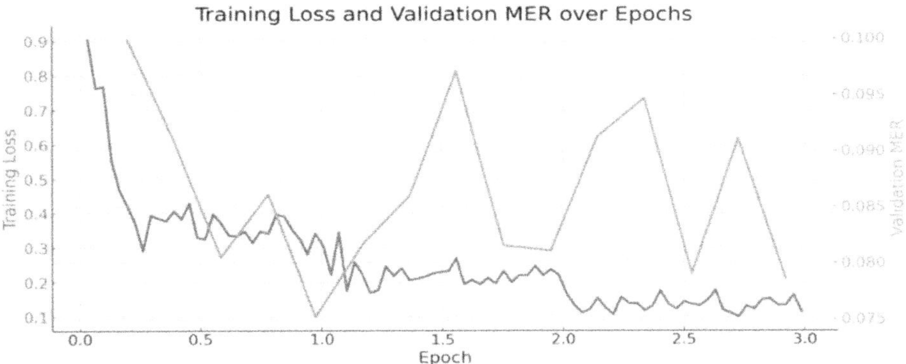

Fig. 3. Training Loss and Validation MER over Epochs.

3.2 Task 2: Sensitive Entity Recognition

Task 2 evaluates both the classification and temporal localization of SHI entities. We report experimental findings from three key perspectives: fine-tuning strategies, alignment methods, and prediction merging.

Model Fine-tuning Comparison: We compared multiple model configurations, including few-shot prompting and QLoRA-based fine-tuning across different instruction-tuned models. Table 3 summarizes the validation F1 scores under each setup. The evaluated models include:

- **Llama-3-Taiwan-8B-Instruct** [15]: a bilingual LLaMA3-based model optimized for Traditional Chinese and English by Yenting Lin.
- **Gemma-3-27B-It (4-bit)** [16]: a 4-bit quantized instruction-tuned version of Google's Gemma-27B, released via Unsloth.
- **Qwen2.5-32B-Instruct** [13]: https://www.authorea.com/users/1010995/articles/137 1101-instruction-tuned-llms-for-multilingual-medical-asr-and-privacy-entity-ext ractiona large multilingual model with strong instruction-following and reasoning capabilities, developed by Alibaba.

In our experiments, the full dataset refers to the combination of official training, validation, and our internally extended samples (see Sect. 2.5). Among all settings, the best validation performance was achieved using QLoRA with per-category fine-tuning on Qwen2.5-32B, as shown in Table 3.

Table 3. Model comparison using different fine-tuning strategies.

Method	Description	Validation F1
Prompting only	Few-shot prompting	0.2049
QLoRA (Llama-3-Taiwan-8B))	Fine-tuned on training dataset	0.4222
QLoRA (Gemma-3-27B)	Fine-tuned on training dataset	0.4807
QLoRA (Qwen2.5-32B, per-type)	Fine-tuned on full dataset	**0.5025**

These results suggest that:

- Fine-tuning substantially improves performance compared to few-shot prompting.
- Using high-capacity models like Qwen2.5-32B with targeted span augmentation leads to optimal results.
- Training separate category-specific sub models provides additional gains, especially for underrepresented Sensitive Health Information (SHI) types.

3.3 Alignment Method Comparison

To map predicted spans to the original audio timestamps, we evaluated three alignment strategies: strict string match, sliding-window, and LLM-based span completion. Table 4 reports their validation F1 scores.

Table 4. Comparison of timestamp alignment strategies.

Method	Description	Validation F1
Strict match	Only exact string matches count	0.2665
Sliding window	Approximate matching by segment	0.5025
LLM-aided matching	Gemini-assisted span completion	0.4565

The sliding-window method achieved the highest accuracy, likely due to its robustness against ASR noise [17]. While LLM-based matching introduces semantic flexibility, it also occasionally over-extends or misinterprets spans. In cases where the sliding window fails to find any string-level match (often due to paraphrasing or heavier ASR drift), the LLM fallback can successfully recover missing spans. Based on this result, we adopted Sliding window + Gemini-assisted as our final method.

3.4 Ensemble Prediction Strategy

To further improve robustness, we explored combining outputs from multiple models [18]. Table 5 compares performance with and without ensemble prediction on the test set.

Table 5. Test F1 scores with and without model ensembling.

Method	Description	Test F1
Single (Qwen2.5-32B)	Fine-tuned on full data	0.3965
Single (Gemma-3-27B)	Fine-tuned on training data	0.4424
Merged (Gemma + Qwen)	Merged by timestamp-aware union	**0.4860**

Our final ensemble strategy merges predictions from both Qwen and Gemma using span-wise alignment and union heuristics. This design increases coverage while maintaining temporal consistency, leading to the highest F1 among all configurations. Thus, we adopted the ensemble as our official submission.

3.5 Error Analysis and Validation

Our best configuration achieves a macro F1 of 0.5025 on the validation set, but the same model drops to 0.3965 on the hidden test set. This sizeable gap indicates a non-trivial generalization issue. To better understand this behavior, we manually inspected a sample of errors and compared the validation and test distributions.

First, the test set contains a higher proportion of long, noisy utterances and more colloquial expressions, leading to larger ASR mismatch between the reference and our Whisper transcripts. Since our timestamp alignment relies on string-level matching, any transcription drift (e.g., paraphrased dates, partially recognized names) directly translates into span-level false negatives even when the underlying entities are semantically correct.

Second, several low-frequency SHI categories (e.g., identifiers and certain location types) are more heavily represented in the test set. These categories are already challenging on the validation set, and the combination of data sparsity and stronger ASR noise amplifies the performance degradation.

Overall, we view this validation–test discrepancy not as an artifact of tuning on the validation set alone, but as evidence that purely text-based span matching is brittle under distribution shift and noisy speech transcripts. We explicitly report this limitation and regard it as an important direction for future work on more robust alignment mechanisms.

4 Discussion

Our results on the AICUP 2025 Spring Challenge highlight the practical effectiveness of instruction-tuned LLMs for SHI extraction from bilingual medical conversations, while also revealing key limitations that affect generalization under noisy ASR conditions.

A central observation is that QLoRA-based fine-tuning consistently outperforms prompting-only baselines by a large margin. This suggests that the SHI extraction task benefits strongly from task-specific adaptation, particularly when the supervision format is aligned with the model's instruction-following capabilities. Among our evaluated settings, category-wise QLoRA fine-tuning on Qwen2.5-32B achieves the strongest validation performance, indicating that targeted training can better mitigate sparsity in low-frequency SHI categories.

We also find that timestamp localization is a decisive factor in end-to-end performance. Strict string-matching leads to a substantial drop in F1 due to its sensitivity to ASR drift, whereas sliding-window alignment provides a better balance between robustness and precision by tolerating small segmentation mismatches. While Gemini-based LLM inference can recover spans when heuristic alignment fails, it may introduce latency and occasionally produces semantically plausible but factually incorrect outputs, making it more suitable as a fallback rather than a primary alignment mechanism.

A major challenge exposed by our experiments is the validation–test performance gap observed in Task 2. Manual inspection suggests this discrepancy is driven by the combined effect of noisier and longer utterances in the test set, increased transcript mismatch from ASR, and a shifted distribution toward rarer SHI categories. Because our alignment pipeline still relies on string-level evidence, even correct semantic predictions may be scored as false negatives if they cannot be precisely grounded to overlapping timestamps. This limitation indicates that improving temporal grounding and reducing alignment brittleness are critical for robust real-world deployment [17].

Language-aware modelling. Our results suggest complementary strengths across model families, where Qwen models may better handle Chinese-centric patterns and Gemma can offer strong instruction-following performance. Future work could integrate language identification and route each utterance through specialized models or language-conditioned adapters.

More robust timestamp alignment. Instead of relying primarily on heuristic sliding windows, future systems could incorporate learned alignment approaches such as span-to-token mapping modules or retrieval-based matching across ASR chunks, enabling greater tolerance to paraphrasing and transcription noise [18].

Joint or multitask training across ASR and SHI extraction. Since entity recognition quality depends heavily on transcription accuracy, tighter integration between ASR and NER—through multitask objectives or shared representations—may reduce error propagation and improve timestamp stability.

Beyond detection, effective de-identification systems must also replace removed SHI with plausible surrogates to maintain contextual realism and downstream data utility using techniques formalized in surrogate generation algorithms for electronic health records [19].

Stronger handling of rare SHI categories. Data augmentation improved coverage, but rare identifier-like categories remain difficult under distribution shift. Future work may explore curriculum sampling, calibrated decoding, or uncertainty-aware postprocessing to improve macro-F1 reliability. These directions represent promising pathways toward building more accurate, temporally grounded, and clinically reliable speech de-identification systems.

5   Conclusion

In this work, we presented our system for the AICUP 2025 Spring Challenge, addressing bilingual medical speech de-identification through a two-stage pipeline consisting of ASR transcription and SHI span extraction with timestamp localization. For ASR, we fine-tuned Whisper-large-v3-turbo separately for Chinese and English speech, achieving strong transcription performance and ranking second in Task 1. For SHI recognition, we reformulated the task into an instruction-based generation format and applied QLoRA fine-tuning to Gemma-3-27B and Qwen2.5-32B, supported by augmentation and category-specific training.

Across our experiments, we showed that instruction-tuned LLM fine-tuning substantially improves SHI extraction compared to prompting-only baselines, and that sliding-window alignment is an effective and scalable strategy for mapping predicted spans back to audio timestamps. Finally, combining predictions from complementary models via span merging improves overall robustness and yields our best end-to-end results. Our final submission ranked sixth overall, demonstrating that instruction tuning combined with hybrid postprocessing provides a practical approach to privacy-aware multilingual medical speech processing.

Acknowledgments. The authors thank the organizers of the AI CUP 2025 competition for providing the official dataset and evaluation platform, which served as the foundation for this research.

Disclosure of Interests The authors declare no competing interests relevant to the content of this article.

References

1. Dai, H.J., et al.: Leveraging large language models for the deidentification and temporal normalization of sensitive health information in electronic health records. npj Digit. Med. **8**(1), 517 (2025)

2. Jonnagaddala, J., Wong, Z.S.-Y.: Privacy preserving strategies for electronic health records in the era of large language models. npj Digit. Med. **8**(1), 34 (2025)
3. Dai, H.J., et al.: A Clinical Speech Corpus with Temporally Aligned Sensitive Health Information (2026). https://www.medrxiv.org/content/10.64898/2026.03.31.26349906v2
4. Panchal, O., et al.: Benchmarking Large Language Models for De-Identification of Electronic Health Record Notes 2026.
5. Dai, H.J., et al.: Leveraging State-of-the-Art LLMs for the De-identification of Sensitive Health Information in Clinical Speech. medRxiv, p. 2026.04.13.26349911 (2026).
6. Jonnagaddala, J., et al.: The OpenDeID corpus for patient de-identification. Sci. Rep. **11**(1), 19973 (2021)
7. Radford, A., et al.: Robust speech recognition via large-scale weak supervision. In: Andreas, K., et al. (eds.) Proceedings of the 40th International Conference on Machine Learning PMLR: Proceedings of Machine Learning Research, pp. 28492–28518 (2023)
8. Wolf, T., et al.: Huggingface's transformers: State-of-the-art natural language processing. arXiv preprint https://arxiv.org/abs/1910.03771 (2019).
9. Alex, C.: Models trained on instruction-following datasets (eg, InstructGPT, Alpaca). 2025.
10. Guo, D., et al.: Deepseek-r1: Incentivizing reasoning capability in llms via reinforcement learning. arXiv preprint https://arxiv.org/abs/2501.12948 (2025).
11. Dettmers, T., et al.: Qlora: efficient finetuning of quantized llms. Adv. Neural Inf. Proces. Syst. **36**, 10088–10115 (2023)
12. Team, G., et al.: Gemma: Open models based on gemini research and technology. arXiv preprint https://arxiv.org/abs/2403.08295 (2024).
13. Yang, Q.A., et al.: Qwen2.5 Technical Report. ArXiv abs/2412.15115 (2024).
14. Team, G., et al.: Gemini: a family of highly capable multimodal models. arXiv preprint https://arxiv.org/abs/2312.11805 (2023).
15. Lin, Y.: Llama-3-Taiwan-8B-Instruct. 2025/07/02. https://huggingface.co/yentinglin/Llama-3-Taiwan-8B-Instruct.
16. Team, G., et al.: Gemma 3 technical report. arXiv preprint https://arxiv.org/abs/2503.19786 (2025)
17. Beltagy, I., M.E. Peters, A. Cohan: Longformer: The long-document transformer. arXiv preprint https://arxiv.org/abs/2004.05150 (2020)
18. Dieterich, T.G.: Ensemble methods in machine learning. In: International Workshop on Multiple Classifier Systems. Springer (2000)
19. Chen, A., et al.: Generation of surrogates for De-identification of electronic health records. Stud. Health Technol. Inform. **264**, 70–73 (2019)

Temporal Subword De-Identification of Medical Speech for Privacy Protection Leveraging ASR and LLMs

Chao-Long Huang[1,2](✉) ⓘ, Pratham Nandy[3] ⓘ, and Hong-Jie Dai[1,2,4,5] ⓘ

[1] Intelligent System Laboratory, Department of Electrical Engineering, College of Electrical Engineering and Computer Science, National Kaohsiung University of Science and Technology, Kaohsiung, Taiwan
austin70915@gmail.com, hjdai@nkust.edu.tw
[2] National Institute of Cancer Research, National Health Research Institutes, Tainan, Taiwan
[3] CGD Health Pvt. Ltd. Mumbai, Hyderabad, India
pratham@cgdhealth.com
[4] School of Post-Baccalaureate Medicine, College of Medicine, Kaohsiung Medical Universi-ty, Kaohsiung, Taiwan
[5] Center for Big Data Research, Kaohsiung Medical University, Kaohsiung, Taiwan

Abstract. This study presents a cross-lingual de-identification framework for medical speech data that integrates Automatic Speech Recognition (ASR) and Large Languages Models (LLMs), validated on a multilingual dataset (Mandarin Chinese, English, and Taiwanese Hokkien). Through systematic experiments, we evaluated the impact of various data sources and fine-tuning strategies on sensitive information identification. Results show that, after initial fine-tuning on Mandarin, even a small amount of domain-specific multilingual data significantly improves de-identification performance compared to using the base model or a single-language fine-tuned model. The proposed approach, incorporating diverse annotation strategies and robust post-processing procedures such as overlap filtering and fuzzy matching, further enhances accuracy and robustness. Importantly, the framework maintains strong performance under limited annotated data, highlighting its potential for real-world clinical data privacy protection and downstream medical AI applications. Future work may extend this framework to additional languages and more complex medical speech contexts, exploring the feasibility and limitations of speech de-identification in specialized clinical domains.

Keywords: Speech De-identification · Large Language Models · Healthcare Privacy · Automatic Speech Recognition · Data Auditing

1 Introduction

As clinical speech datasets continue to grow at scale, constructing reliable and reusable medical corpora without compromising patient privacy has become a pressing challenge [1]. In multilingual clinical speech, code-switching, dialectal variation, and ASR artifacts make boundary control and long-tail entities particularly challenging for de-identification.

© The Author(s), under exclusive license to Springer Nature Singapore Pte Ltd. 2026
J. Jonnagaddala et al. (Eds.): IW-DMRN 2025, CCIS 2908, pp. 15–27, 2026.
https://doi.org/10.1007/978-981-92-2282-7_2

In multilingual healthcare settings such as Taiwan, where Mandarin, English, and Taiwanese Hokkien frequently intermingle in spontaneous speech, identifying and masking sensitive entities (e.g., names, dates, addresses, and institutional identifiers) becomes significantly more complex. Traditional approaches struggle with ASR-generated transcription errors, which often distort code-switching patterns, dialect-specific expressions, and specialized medical terminology. These artifacts introduce substantial noise, degrading training data quality and impairing downstream model performance.

Recent LLM capabilities can be leveraged to strengthen clinical de-identification by enabling context-aware detection of sensitive health information beyond rule-based matching. A key advantage of their approach is integrating **temporal** normalization alongside de-identification, reducing privacy leakage from dates and time expressions while maintaining clinical timeline coherence [2]. Overall, the paper highlights a scalable direction for privacy-preserving health data processing where LLMs improve robustness to diverse writing styles and edge cases, reminding that effective protection requires both identity removal and control of temporal linkage signals. We propose an NER-based de-identification approach that achieves competitive performance in the AI CUP 2025 Spring setting, enabling more reliable processing of sensitive information in medical speech data. The proposed method adopts a two-stage, dataset-level enhancement strategy normalization and LLM-assisted labeling to improve annotation consistency and recall within a semantics-aware alignment and rule-verified masking pipeline. First, transcript-level normalization mitigates inconsistencies caused by multilingual interference, dialectal variation, and ASR-induced entity distortion through terminology standardization, dialect alignment, and transcription error correction. Second, LLM-assisted annotation augments and refines labels by using contextual understanding to detect sensitive entities that are often missed by rule-based heuristics or limited training data, particularly low-frequency or underrepresented mentions such as rare surnames, local clinic names, small-town addresses, or uncommon institutional abbreviations. This helps reduce false negatives and improves consistency in boundary selection for multi-token spans, which is critical for high-quality de-identification datasets. As a result, the annotation process achieves broader label coverage and higher recall, while also supporting faster iteration of the annotation schema by surfacing new entity variants that may not have been captured in the original guidelines [3].

The proposed framework combines ASR-based preprocessing and LLM-assisted semantic enrichment to improve dataset consistency and the robustness of downstream de-identification systems in low-resource, multilingual settings. On the AI CUP 2025 Spring tasks, the pipeline achieves competitive performance and reduces boundary errors and false positives, while long-tail labels and noisy segments remain challenging.

2   Methods

This study adopts a bimodal, two-stage pipeline. First, spoken audio is transcribed into text; second, the text undergoes NER-based detection and masking of sensitive content. CrisperWhisper and FireRedASR are combined in the speech-to-text stage, followed by Qwen3-14B for SHI detection and direct masking to preserve privacy. The workflow is: speech - text - entity recognition - masking. To address conversational data issues such as breaks or omissions, a recursive inference mechanism semantically completes missing fragments. During NER training, a sliding window captures feature distributions under truncated contexts, followed by full-text inference to restore broader context. Explicit constraints are imposed to prevent runaway semantic extension.

2.1 Dataset

The study uses the SREDH-AICup SHI speech corpus 2025 which is constructed using OpenDeID v2 corpus dataset. The original OpenDeID v2 corpus consists of text-based electronic medical records (EMRs) intended for text de-identification tasks, with no associated speech data [4]. Building on this foundation, OpenDeID v2 was adapted for the current competition through additional preprocessing and transformation procedures to construct a speech-oriented dataset from the original text reports. A subset of EMR reports was randomly sampled and rewritten into recording scripts by two domain specialists according to the SHI annotation categories. These scripts were then recorded by 25 speakers from the College of Foreign Languages, National Kaohsiung University of Science and Technology (NKUST), comprising 9 males and 16 females, where each speaker contributed approximately 10 to 20 audio samples [5].

2.2 Data Processing Pipeline

Our data preprocessing pipeline processes raw audio–text pairs with a preliminary model, producing a cleaned, aligned training set for the primary model. For English audio, we adopt the CrisperWhisper [6] model, while FireRedASR-AED [7] serves as the core engine for Mandarin, particularly for correcting low-quality ASR labels. The workflow is organized into three stages, each incorporating quality-control mechanisms to ensure data usability, accuracy, and stability.

Alignment: A model trained raw data generates initial transcriptions using greedy decoding to reduce error rates. These transcriptions are then used to identify and discard highly erroneous sentences, often resulting from misaligned segments or incorrect annotations common in competition datasets.

Expansion: Temperature fallback is applied to generate diverse alternatives for poorly transcribed segments, producing samples within an acceptable risk margin while preserving usability.

Convergence: Refinement involves retraining the model on processed data and decoding with beam search to improve fluency, semantic consistency, and boundary precision. Discarded samples are reprocessed with the updated model and added to the final training set.

Audio files are converted to mono with a unified sampling rate, and segments shorter than 0.5 s, longer than 30 s, or containing abnormal silence are removed. Language identification combines metadata and automatic recognition, with ambiguous cases retained to prevent accidental deletion. Text normalization is language-specific: English transcriptions are lowercased, with basic punctuation retained and spelling or code-switching errors corrected; Chinese transcriptions are converted from Traditional to Simplified Chinese. Superfluous symbols and formatting issues are removed to ensure consistency.

Quality assessment uses Word Error Rate (WER) and Character Error Rate (CER) to measure speech–text alignment, supplemented by structural metrics such as punctuation density, average token length, and subword diversity. Filters are dynamically adjusted based on dataset distributions to balance discarding errors against preserving useful data. The architecture is structured, reproducible, and scalable, enhancing data quality and accelerating model training in the short term, reducing manual labeling costs in the medium term, and improving reusability and risk control in the long term. Limitations include the reliance on WER and CER as proxies without human-labeled ground truth and residual transcription errors despite high-temperature generation. Future work will explore fine-grained semantic evaluation, speaker-style normalization, and active learning for edge cases.

2.3 Addressing Crosstalk Alignment

After processing the ASR dataset, inconsistencies in timestamp and label alignment between Task 1 and Task 2 were observed, mainly due to missing words or imprecise labels. To align with Task 2 requirements, basic alignment and data cleaning were performed, using greedy decoding for baseline stability. The trained model was then applied to regenerate samples with remaining label discrepancies, correcting formatting errors (e.g., "10 PM" $\rightarrow$ "ten PM") and semantic deviations caused by tense changes.

Because the initial model was preliminary, some automatically generated labels lacked precision. Low-confidence samples were removed, and a language model was retrained on the cleaned dataset. For large-scale processing, Qwen3-8B [8] improved throughput and reduced manual annotation, while Qwen3-14B generated the final refined labels. Leveraging advanced LLM comprehension, missing labels were recovered and earlier annotation errors corrected, enhancing dataset accuracy and completeness. Refinement focused primarily on English data; Chinese relied on the model's built-in language understanding without additional optimization.

2.4 ASR Model Choice & Word-Level Alignment

CrisperWhisper is used to obtain precise word-level timestamps, feeding decoder cross-attention scores into a Dynamic Time Warping (DTW) algorithm for fine-grained alignment between speech frames and tokens with up to 25 ms resolution. *Softmax* normalization calibrates each acoustic frame's contribution to the current token, enhancing stability. To prevent DTW from spreading alignment errors over long pauses, any pause exceeding 160 ms is evenly distributed to the preceding and following words (e.g., a 200 ms pause allocates 100 ms to each side; see Algorithm 1).

Algorithm 1 Adjust Pause Distribution

Require: blocks Sequence of aligned timestamp blocks

Require: threshold Redistribution pause threshold (160 ms)

1	function ADJUST_PAUSE(blocks, threshold)
2	if blocks is empty then
3	return blocks
4	end if
5	adjusted_blocks ← a deep copy of blocks
6	for each pair of consecutive blocks (current, next) do
7	(cs, ce) ← start and end time of current block
8	(ns, ne) ← start and end time of next block
9	pause_duration ← ns − ce
10	if pause_duration > 0 then
11	if pause_duration > threshold then
12	allocation ← threshold / 2
13	else
14	allocation ← pause_duration / 2
15	end if
16	Update current block's end time: ce ← ce + allocation
17	Update next block's start time: ns ← ns − allocation
18	end if
19	end for
20	return adjusted_blocks
21	end function

The speech recognition engine uses *FireRedASR*, an attention-based encoder–decoder (AED) model. Its encoder employs a Conformer structure, combining CNN modules for local acoustic features with self-attention for global semantics. Two front-end convolutional layers reduce computation while preserving key cues. Fixed positional encoding and shared input/output embeddings compress parameters. Input features are 80-dimensional log-Mel filter banks with 25 ms windows and 10 ms hop size. Each self-attention layer is flanked by Macaron-style feed-forward networks before and after, enhancing semantic learning.

2.5 ASR Training Strategy

A progressive regularization schedule is adopted: early phases omit regularization to allow rapid structural learning, then Dropout and *SpecAugment* are gradually introduced to enhance robustness. Empirically, this schedule benefits both large and lightweight models.

Architecturally, Whisper is modified by pruning the Value (V) vectors in the encoder while retaining Query (Q) and Key (K). Since ASR focuses on acoustic-semantic alignment rather than long-sequence generation, removing V reduces semantic interference, sharpens feature matching, and lowers computational cost. The decoder retains full Q, K, and V to preserve generation capability. Excluding V in the encoder helps the model focus on acoustic-semantic alignment, improving generalization on sensitive items such as names and addresses.

All audio inputs are standardized to 16 kHz mono, and time-axis prediction is disabled. For English data, the Beginning of Sentence Token is removed to improve cross-language consistency. Data augmentation uses dynamic scheduling, automatically tuning augmentation strength based on validation loss to prevent overfitting. Techniques include time shifting, background-noise injection, frequency masking, and volume perturbation, enhancing robustness to noisy signals. Due to limited Chinese speech data, a weighted random sampler up-weights underrepresented labels. All parameters are fine-tuned (LoRA is not used), and the best model is selected based on validation loss for deployment.

2.6 NER Model Architecture & Selection

For NER, Qwen3-14B Base is used as the backbone. It features Rotary Positional Embedding (RoPE) [9], Grouped Query Attention (GQA) [10], and QKNorm [11], and is pretrained on a large corpus. Its strong semantic understanding and reasoning in mid-to-large tasks suit our scenario. Pretraining involves Mixture-of-Experts training for reasoning, Reinforcement Learning, fine-tuning for generation, optional "Thinking" mode for long chain-of-thought reasoning, and knowledge distillation to compress the model while preserving performance. These features support low-label settings requiring robust semantic modeling.

2.7 NER Training Protocols

A two-stage fine-tuning strategy is adopted with NEFtune (Noise Embedded Fine-tuning) [12]. NEFtune attaches a forward hook to the embedding layer and injects small random noise during training, enhancing robustness to natural input variations, particularly under low-data conditions.

Stage 1: Non-SHI segments are filtered or down sampled to prevent the model from learning trivial patterns and reduce annotation noise. Tokenization is performed with spaCy, and sliding windows simulate discontinuous contexts. About 10% of non-SHI segments are retained to maintain class balance. Loss is computed only on entity-tag predictions, focusing learning on relevant portions, which is critical for small datasets.

Stage 2: After initial discrimination, fine-tuning is performed on the full dataset while retaining ~30% of the most representative samples. This emphasizes key semantic patterns and mitigates overfitting to redundant structures.

Algorithm 2: Word-Level Alignment with Normalization
Require: w: Target entity word/phrase
Require: s: Search start index
Require: words: List of word objects containing timestamps
Require: T: Transcription tokens from ASR
Require: used: Set of indices already assigned to other entities

```
1    function ALIGN_ONCE(w, s, words, T, used)
2       q ← TOKENIZE(w)
3       if |q| = 0 then
4          return None
5       end if
6       for i ← s to |T| − |q| do
7          match ← True
8          for k ← 0 to |q| − 1 do
9             if NORMALIZE(T[i + k].token) ≠ NORMALIZE(q[k]) then
10               match ← False
11               break
12            end if
13         end for
14         if match then
15            a ← T[i].index, b ← T[i + |q| − 1].index
16            pos ← {i, ..., i + |q| − 1}
17            if pos ∩ used = ∅ then
18               used ← used ∪ pos
19               return (words[a].start, words[b].end, i + 1)
20            end if
21         end if
22      end for
23      return None
24   end function
```

2.8 Integrated Semantic-Time Processing Pipeline

An integrated semantic-time pipeline aligns NER outputs with word-level timestamps for bilingual Chinese English speech. Each identified entity is mapped to its corresponding acoustic segment, supporting redaction, information extraction, and conversational analytics. Model predictions are generated as SHI word pairs, with each word tagged by entity type. For English inputs, token-to-word mappings are created with the spaCy tokenizer and aligned to Crisper Whisper's timestamped token stream using Algorithm 2. Additional pre-processing handles tokenization inconsistencies (e.g., normalization), and post-processing assigns precise start and end times to each entity. For Chinese inputs, character-level mappings align directly to CrisperWhisper's character-timed outputs. Multi-character entities are treated as unified spans with aggregated timing. To resolve conflicts from repeated or overlapping annotations, a long-span priority strategy retains the tag covering the broader context, using confidence scores or shallow contextual re-evaluation for exact overlaps. A minimum temporal separation between adjacent entities ensures distinct time-stamp boundaries in rapid or noisy speech. Results are compiled into structured JSON containing original text, per-character timestamps, entity spans and types, and optionally a privacy-masked version, supporting anonymization, evaluation, and human review in multilingual and code-switched datasets.

3   Experimental Results

3.1   Performance for Validation Set

In AI CUP 2025 Spring, Task 1 evaluated speech alignment using Mixed Error Rate (MER), and Task 2 assessed entity recognition with masking (macro-averaged precision, recall, and F1). On the validation set, character-level MER was 0.0554, reflecting stable alignment achieved through DTW calibration and long-pause redistribution. Multi-turn interruptions or variable speech rates largely maintained boundary consistency, though pauses over 160 ms occasionally caused minor token-boundary diffusion. MER degradation was primarily due to speech heterogeneity: test data included colloquial Chinese, numeric code-switching, and Taiwanese vocabulary, diverging from training corpora. *FireRedASR* attention sometimes shifted alignment boundaries, suggesting future fine-tuning should expand dialectal and mixed-language coverage to improve robustness.

For Task 2 (Entity Recognition), the NER model achieved macro-average Precision 0.7785, Recall 0.8619, and F1-score 0.8128 (N = 2,037, Table 1). Structured entities such as DATE, ID_NUMBER, and MEDICAL_RECORD_NUMBER performed best (F1 > 0.91). CITY and SET were moderate, while LOCATION-OTHER was weakest (F1 = 0.2156) due to sparse data and ambiguous semantics. Misclassifications occurred mainly in compound entities (e.g., "XX Hospital Internal Medicine Department") where boundaries between HOSPITAL and DEPARTMENT blurred. Semantic overlap in Chinese (CITY, STATE, COUNTY, DISTRICT) caused label swaps, especially for under-represented categories. Two-stage fine-tuning with NEFtune improved stable categories, but ambiguous classes like LOCATION-OTHER still suffered from low recall. Results are demonstrated in Table 1.

3.2   Test Performance

On the test set, Task 1 (MER) rose to 0.1293, indicating weaker alignment under more complex speech, likely due to increased Chinese content, variable recording quality, and code-switching, which affected FireRedASR attention stability. For Task 2 (NER), the model achieved macro-averaged Precision 0.7174, Recall 0.7580, and F1 0.7103 (N = 3,404, Table 2). Despite the overall decline, DATE and TIME remained strong due to normalization and rule-based validation.

Chinese subsets were more volatile, especially PERSONALNAME and FAMILY-NAME, where colloquial variation and segmentation errors appeared to reduce accuracy (with small supports for these categories). For instance, "name + title" was often treated

Table 1. Validation Set Results by Entity Type

SHI Category	Precision	Recall	F-Measure	Support
PATIENT	0.7914	0.9095	0.8463	182
DOCTOR	0.8275	0.9090	0.8663	306
PERSONALNAME	0.5659	0.7658	0.6508	46
FAMILYNAME	0.7063	0.9000	0.7915	28
PROFESSION	0.5294	0.7643	0.6255	14
DEPARTMENT	0.8702	0.8711	0.8707	67
HOSPITAL	0.8840	0.8784	0.8812	73
ORGANIZATION	0.9184	0.8801	0.8989	12
STREET	0.8161	0.9338	0.8710	64
CITY	0.7606	0.8915	0.8209	65
STATE	0.8611	0.9423	0.8999	64
COUNTRY	0.7027	0.9158	0.7952	3
COUNTY	0.6971	1.0000	0.8215	2
ZIP	0.8691	0.8766	0.8728	60
LOCATION-OTHER	0.3367	0.1586	0.2156	6
DISTRICT	0.8303	0.9133	0.8698	1
AGE	0.8889	0.7776	0.8295	17
DATE	0.8990	0.9322	0.9153	493
TIME	0.8289	0.8708	0.8493	110
DURATION	0.7109	0.9201	0.8021	152
SET	0.7307	0.9305	0.8186	29
MEDICAL_RECORD_NUMBER	0.9368	0.9510	0.9438	68
ID_NUMBER	0.9430	0.9318	0.9374	175
macro-avg.	**0.7785**	**0.8619**	**0.8128**	**2037**

as a single entity, and "Mr. Li" was misclassified as PATIENT. Error patterns differed by entity. PROFESSION showed high recall (0.9484) but low precision (0.3952), indicating boundary overextension. ROOM showed high precision (0.8661) but low recall (0.4342), indicating under-detection. COUNTRY suffered from contextual ambiguity (e.g., "US pharmaceutical company" misclassified as ORGANIZATION). LOCATION-OTHER achieved high precision (0.9632) but low recall (0.455) due to stringent filtering, reflecting a quality-versus-coverage tradeoff.

Strengths included consistent temporal entities (DATE, TIME) and the benefits of schema constraints for cross-domain stability. Weaknesses centered on rare or long-tail labels (PERSONALNAME, FAMILYNAME), boundary control for PROFESSION,

Table 2. Test Set Results by Entity Type

SHI Category	Precision	Recall	F-Measure	Support
PATIENT	0.7474	0.8989	0.8162	468
DOCTOR	0.8146	0.9114	0.8603	832
PERSONALNAME	0.0566	0.4458	0.1005	4
FAMILYNAME	0.0397	0.0457	0.0425	12
PROFESSION	0.3952	0.9484	0.5579	2
ROOM	0.8661	0.4342	0.5784	2
DEPARTMENT	0.7920	0.8848	0.8358	135
HOSPITAL	0.8790	0.8073	0.8416	167
ORGANIZATION	0.9549	0.7924	0.8661	6
STREET	0.8355	0.8688	0.8518	116
CITY	0.7825	0.7869	0.7847	120
STATE	0.8394	0.8987	0.8681	111
COUNTRY	0.5451	0.9350	0.6887	2
ZIP	0.8814	0.8325	0.8562	115
LOCATION-OTHER	0.9632	0.4550	0.6180	4
AGE	0.8678	0.7157	0.7844	34
DATE	0.9508	0.9336	0.9421	650
TIME	0.8885	0.9146	0.9014	125
DURATION	0.3245	0.7929	0.4605	8
SET	0.2235	0.3623	0.2764	8
MEDICAL_RECORD_NUMBER	0.9686	0.8294	0.8936	158
ID_NUMBER	0.9265	0.9402	0.9333	324
macro-avg.	**0.7174**	**0.7580**	**0.7103**	**3404**

cautious detection of ROOM, schema-induced ambiguity for COUNTRY, and precision-favoring filters that reduced LOCATION-OTHER recall.

Table 2 shows the results for all entity types.

4 Discussion

4.1 System Performance and Strengths

This study presents an auditable end-to-end de-identification pipeline for medical conversations, combining ASR, LLM-based NER, and rule-based validation. The system ranked third in Task 1 and first in Task 2 at AI CUP 2025 Spring, reflecting methodological robustness and practical applicability. While boundary diffusion persists under variable audio conditions, time-related and encoded entities were reliably identified. Challenges remain with Chinese long-tail entities and ambiguous boundaries. Expanding linguistic coverage, improving annotation consistency, and applying targeted training could raise macro-F1 by ~10% to 0.78. Enhancing recall and boundary precision while minimizing over- and under-redaction will strengthen audit readiness and adaptability across clinical and insurance domains without increasing operational complexity.

4.2 Ethical, Legal and Practical Considerations

Medical speech de-identification is both a technical step and an ethical requirement. Clinical conversations may contain protected health information [2](PHI) that can directly reveal identity of individuals (e.g., names, phone numbers, addresses) or indirectly enable re-identification through contextual cues [13]. Previous clinical de-identification work has highlighted that conversational content can increase re-identification [14] risk due to the accumulation of seemingly benign details across time. This makes robust sensitive information detection essential for safe data sharing and research use [15]. A key privacy challenge in speech-based clinical data is that identifiers may appear in inconsistent or non-standard forms due to hesitations, corrections, dialectal pronunciation, and transcription variability introduced by ASR. This motivates the use of hybrid pipelines that combine model-based identification with post-processing strategies to reduce missed identifiers and inconsistent masking, aligning with findings that hybrid de-identification approaches can improve reliability across PHI categories [16]. Importantly, de-identification must balance privacy protection with clinical utility [17]. Over-redaction may remove medically relevant information, while under-redaction can leave residual identifiers that can compromise confidentiality of the data. This trade-off has been widely recognized in clinical text de-identification and becomes more complex in multilingual environments where names and institutions may appear across languages or scripts [18]. Finally, speech recordings may carry additional privacy risks beyond transcript content, including potential re-identification from voice characteristics. Recent evidence indicates that re-identification risk in shared clinical speech datasets is a practical concern, reinforcing the need to treat de-identification as a risk-reduction strategy rather than a guarantee of anonymity [19]. Findings are supported by a comprehensive multi-dataset benchmarking analysis that contrasts rule-based, hybrid, and LLM-based methods across heterogeneous electronic health record corpora.

5 Conclusion

This study developed an auditable end-to-end de-identification pipeline for multilingual medical conversations by integrating ASR-based transcription, sensitive entity detection and rule-based validation to improve reliability and consistency. Competitive performance in AI CUP 2025 Spring demonstrates the system's practical strength for real-world privacy protection scenarios. While challenges remain, the framework offers a robust foundation for deployment due to its modular design and strong performance on structured identifier categories. Future work will focus on improving boundary precision and recall through targeted training, expanded linguistic coverage, and more consistent annotation practices, aiming to enhance macro-F1 without increasing operational complexity. Overall, the proposed approach supports scalable, accountable de-identification for sensitive conversational data, enabling safer clinical data sharing and medical AI applications.

Acknowledgments. This study was supported in part by the National Institute of Cancer Research, National Health Research Institutes, Tainan, Taiwan, and the Center for Big Data Research at Kaohsiung Medical University. The authors would like to thank the organizers of the AI CUP 2025 Spring competition for providing the dataset and the evaluation platform that made this research possible.

Disclosure of Interests. The authors have no competing interests to declare that are relevant to the content of this article.

References

1. Dai, H.J., et al.: Leveraging State-of-the-Art LLMs for the De-identification of Sensitive Health Information in Clinical Speech. medRxiv, p. 2026.04.13.26349911 (2026).
2. Dai, H.J., et al.: Leveraging large language models for the deidentification and temporal normalization of sensitive health information in electronic health records. npj Digit. Med. **8**(1), 517 (2025)
3. Panchal, O., et al.: Benchmarking Large Language Models for De-identification of Electronic Health Record Notes (2026).
4. Jonnagaddala, J., et al.: The OpenDeID corpus for patient de-identification. Sci. Rep. **11**(1), 19973 (2021)
5. Dai, H.J., et al.: A Clinical Speech Corpus with Temporally Aligned Sensitive Health Information (2026). https://www.medrxiv.org/content/10.64898/2026.03.31.26349906v2
6. Yang, A., et al.: Qwen3 technical report. arXiv preprint https://arxiv.org/abs/2505.09388 (2025).
7. Wagner, L., B. Thallinger, M. Zusag: Crisperwhisper: Accurate timestamps on verbatim speech transcriptions. arXiv preprint https://arxiv.org/abs/2408.16589 (2024).
8. Xu, K.T., et al.: Fireredasr: Open-source industrial-grade mandarin speech recognition models from encoder-decoder to llm integration. arXiv preprint https://arxiv.org/abs/2501.14350 (2025).
9. Su, J., et al.: RoFormer: enhanced transformer with rotary position embedding. Neurocomputing. **568**, 127063 (2024)
10. Hudson, D.A., Manning, C.D.: Gqa: a new dataset for real-world visual reasoning and compositional question answering. In: Proceedings of the IEEE/CVF Conference on Computer Vision and Pattern Recognition (2019)
11. Henry, A., et al.: Query-key normalization for transformers. In: Findings of the Association for Computational Linguistics: EMNLP 2020 (2020)
12. Jain, N., et al.: Neftune: Noisy embeddings improve instruction finetuning. arXiv preprint https://arxiv.org/abs/2310.05914 (2023)
13. Jonnagaddala, J., Wong, Z.S.Y.: Privacy preserving strategies for electronic health records in the era of large language models. npj Digit. Med. **8**(1), 34 (2025)
14. Jonnagaddala, J. and S.T. Liaw, Chapter 11 - addressing challenges with implementing essential digital tools. In: Digital Health Maturity: Quality, Interoperability, and Innovation, S.T. Liaw, et al. (Eds.), Academic. pp. 265–276 2026.

15. Stubbs, A., Kotfila, C., Uzuner, O.: Automated systems for the de-identification of longitudinal clinical narratives: overview of 2014 i2b2/UTHealth shared task track 1. J. Biomed. Inform. **58**(Suppl), S11–S19 (2015)
16. Liu, Z., et al.: Automatic de-identification of electronic medical records using token-level and character-level conditional random fields. J. Biomed. Inform. **58**, S47–S52 (2015)
17. Chen, A., et al.: Generation of surrogates for De-identification of electronic health records. Stud. Health Technol. Inform. **264**, 70–73 (2019)
18. Negash, B., et al.: De-identification of free text data containing personal health information: a scoping review of reviews. Int. J. Popul Data Sci. **8**(1), 2153 (2023)
19. Wiepert, D., et al.: Reidentification of participants in shared clinical data sets: experimental study. JMIR AI. **3**, e52054 (2024)

Prompt Engineering and Post-Processing for Sensitive Health Information Recognition

Ming-Chan Lee[1] ⓘ, Liang-Kai Chen[1(✉)] ⓘ, and Yu-Jie Huang[2] ⓘ

[1] Department of Electrical Engineering, National Kaohsiung University of Science and Technology, Kaohsiung 80778, Taiwan
{mclee,c111154102}@nkust.edu.tw
[2] Department of Cross College Elite Tech Program, National Kaohsiung University of Science and Technology, Kaohsiung 81157, Taiwan
c111196104@nkust.edu.tw

Abstract. This study proposes an automated pipeline for de-identifying sensitive health information from doctor–patient voice recordings by integrating automatic speech recognition, large language models, prompt engineering, and post-processing techniques. The proposed system combines OpenAI's Whisper for transcription, WhisperX for word-level alignment and speaker diarization, and GPT-4-Turbo with structured prompts for SHI extraction. The proposed pipeline supports both English and Chinese and produces structured outputs with precise timestamps. Addressing real-world challenges such as hallucinations, entity misclassification, and formatting errors through iterative prompt refinement and tailored post-processing, our approach significantly improves SHI extraction accuracy. This practical solution advances the application of artificial-intelligence-driven clinical natural language processing for analyzing unstructured multilingual voice data.

Keywords: Sensitive health information (SHI) · Automatic speech recognition (ASR) · Prompt engineering

1 Introduction

1.1 Background and Significance

The rapid digitization of healthcare has revolutionized the processing, storage, and analysis of sensitive health information (SHI). Doctor–patient voice conversations, which are rich in clinical insights but inherently unstructured, are among the most critical sources of SHI. These conversations typically contain protected health information (PHI), such as patient names, medical conditions, and demographic details, making them subject to stringent privacy regulations such as the Health Insurance Portability and Accountability Act (HIPAA) in the United States. Ensuring compliance with these regulations while preserving the utility of the data for research and clinical applications is a significant challenge [1, 2].

© The Author(s), under exclusive license to Springer Nature Singapore Pte Ltd. 2026
J. Jonnagaddala et al. (Eds.): IW-DMRN 2025, CCIS 2908, pp. 28–43, 2026.
https://doi.org/10.1007/978-981-92-2282-7_3

Voice data present unique challenges compared with text-based SHI. Unlike structured electronic health records (EHRs), voice data require transcription, speaker identification, and contextual understanding before they can be analyzed. Furthermore, voice is a biometric identifier that adds another layer of complexity to de-identification efforts. The sensitivity of these data highlights the need for robust systems that can process, analyze, and de-identify voice conversations while maintaining compliance with privacy standards [3, 4].

1.2 Literature Context

Conventional clinical de-identification research has largely focused on text-based data, rule-based systems, and supervised machine learning models. Although effective in structured scenarios, these methods struggle with the ambiguity and variability present in unstructured clinical narratives, particularly overlapping entities, institution-specific abbreviations, and polysemous medical terms [5–7].

In voice-based SHI processing, automatic speech recognition (ASR) quality is fundamental. Multilingual ASR systems such as Whisper and WhisperX have demonstrated strong performance in cross-lingual clinical environments. Notably, fine-tuning these models multilingually has led to significant gains in Mandarin medical contexts. This fidelity is crucial given that downstream SHI extraction directly depends on accurate transcription [8, 9].

A major challenge highlighted in the recent MEDINFO literature is that approximately 80% of EHR content remains unstructured, making reliable extraction of computable entities difficult. This challenge is intensified in multilingual settings in which comprehensive non-English medical terminologies are limited. To address this issue, workflows such as translate–align–extract–normalize leverage rich English-based ontologies through translation–alignment techniques to improve multilingual clinical named entity recognition (NER) performance [10].

In addition to extraction accuracy, interoperability remains a critical issue. The HL7 FHIR standard is increasingly adopted to transform unstructured narratives, such as pathology reports, into structured observation resources, thereby enabling standardized clinical information exchange [11]. Consequently, SHI de-identification systems must not only remove identifiers but also produce structured outputs compatible with such interoperability standards.

Finally, recent medical informatics discourse extends the FAIR — Findable, Accessible, Interoperable, and Reusable — principles by introducing reliability (FAIR+R), emphasizing the correctness and semantic specificity of extracted data. Techniques such as constrained large language model (LLM) prompting and post-processing validation play an essential role in achieving these reliability requirements [12].

1.3 System Context

This study proposes a practical pipeline for the de-identification of SHI from doctor–patient voice conversations, leveraging state-of-the-art technologies. The proposed system integrates OpenAI's Whisper and WhisperX for transcription and word-level alignment and speaker diarization, respectively. These tools provide accurate timestamps and speaker attribution, which are essential for downstream processing. For SHI extraction, GPT-4-Turbo is employed, utilizing structured prompts to identify and redact PHI. The proposed pipeline supports multilingual inputs, including English and Chinese, and generates structured outputs suitable for clinical and research applications [8, 9].

The modular design of the proposed system allows for flexibility and scalability. Whisper handles transcription with high accuracy, while WhisperX addresses limitations in timestamp precision and speaker identification. GPT-4-Turbo ensures context-aware extraction of sensitive entities, guided by prompt engineering. This combination of tools represents a significant advancement in the processing of unstructured voice data, bridging the gap between transcription and de-identification.

1.4 Real-World Challenges

De-identification of clinical data has been extensively investigated in the context of written EHR narratives. Early work relied primarily on rule-based systems, using predefined patterns, dictionaries, and handcrafted rules to detect HIPAA-defined PHI categories. Classic systems, such as those proposed by Neamatullah et al., have demonstrated competitive performance on institution-specific datasets but require extensive manual maintenance and lack portability across domains [13].

To improve scalability, supervised machine learning approaches have been proposed, most notably conditional random fields (CRFs), which treat the de-identification task as a sequence-labeling problem. These models integrate lexical and contextual features and generally outperform rule-based methods even though they are heavily dependent on large annotated corpora and require retraining for new institutions or languages [14].

Subsequent work has adopted deep learning-based methods, such as BiLSTM–CRF architectures and later transformer-based clinical NER models. These approaches improve the handling of long-range dependencies and rare PHI categories, but they still assume well-structured written text and do not directly address the variability of spoken clinical dialogue [15, 16].

The most widely used baseline for speech-based de-identification is the two-stage "ASR + NER" pipeline. In this setup, an ASR system generates transcripts, after which a text-based NER model (e.g., CRF, BiLSTM, or BERT) identifies PHI in the text. Cohn et al. formalized this as "audio de-identification", where recognized PHI spans must be mapped back to the audio stream for masking [17]. Although practical, this baseline has several inherited limitations: transcription errors propagate to downstream NER, timestamps are typically unavailable or inaccurate, and multilingual or code-switched speech remains difficult to process. As discussed in recent evaluations, such pipelines primarily serve as lower-bound baselines rather than fully adequate solutions for real-world conversational data [18].

In automated de-identification pipelines for electronic health records (EHRs), the removal of protected health information (PHI) is often followed by the generation of surrogate values that replace the identified identifiers while preserving the structural and contextual integrity of the clinical text. Surrogate generation enables clinical documents to remain realistic and usable for downstream research tasks without exposing identifiable patient information. Chen et al. proposed an algorithmic approach for generating realistic surrogates in unstructured EHR data, allowing sensitive identifiers to be replaced with synthetic placeholders that maintain the linguistic characteristics of the original records [19]. This approach supports the development of automated de-identification systems while ensuring patient privacy and facilitating safe sharing of clinical datasets for research and model development.

Several additional challenges emerged in our system implementation. Hallucination in LLM outputs, where fabricated content is generated despite not being present in the audio, poses a notable risk to extraction reliability and requires iterative prompt engineering to mitigate [3, 4]. Entity-type ambiguity, including confusion between personal and family names, further complicates SHI extraction and aligns with limitations noted in previous clinical NER research [5, 6] These issues highlight the need for a more integrated, speech-aware de-identification pipeline capable of handling transcription variability, multilingual dialogue, alignment errors, and LLM reliability concerns simultaneously.

1.5 Research Goals and Contributions

This study aims to advance the field of clinical natural language processing by demonstrating a practical pipeline for the de-identification of SHI from voice conversations. The primary contributions of this work are as follows:

1. **System Design:** We present a modular pipeline that integrates Whisper, WhisperX, and GPT-4-Turbo, demonstrating its ability to process multilingual inputs and generate structured outputs with precise timestamps.
2. **Error Mitigation:** We address common challenges in ASR + LLM pipelines, including hallucination, entity-type ambiguity, and format parsing errors, through iterative prompt engineering and post-processing strategies.
3. **Privacy Compliance:** By aligning the system with HIPAA standards and leveraging recent advancements in privacy-preserving NER frameworks, we ensure secure processing of sensitive clinical data [1, 2].
4. **Actionable Insights:** We provide comprehensive analysis of the system's performance and challenges, offering guidelines for deploying artificial-intelligence-driven de-identification solutions in healthcare settings.

By grounding our implementation in both system design and literature-driven practices, this study contributes to the growing body of research on AI applications in healthcare, emphasizing the importance of technical performance, scalability, and regulatory integrity.

2 Method

2.1 Dataset

The experiments in this study utilize the SREDH-AICup SHI speech corpus 2025, a benchmark dataset constructed using OpenDeID v2 Corpus which was released by the SREDH Consortium [20] and used in the SREDH/AI Cup 2025 [21] for evaluating automated de-identification systems. The corpus contains 2,100 oncology-related pathology reports from 1,833 cancer patients, with an average length of approximately 700 tokens per document. Across the dataset, 38,414 protected health information (PHI) entities are manually annotated, providing a comprehensive benchmark for sensitive health information recognition tasks. The annotations were created by expert annotators with a reported inter-annotator agreement of approximately 0.94, indicating high labeling reliability [22]. To ensure privacy protection, all identifiable patient information in the dataset is replaced with synthetic surrogate values, allowing the corpus to preserve realistic clinical language patterns while preventing disclosure of real patient identities.

2.2 Privacy and De-Identification Considerations

The increasing use of electronic health records (EHRs) for research and clinical analytics has amplified the need for reliable mechanisms to identify and protect sensitive health information (SHI) embedded in clinical narratives. Recent studies have shown that large language models (LLMs) can effectively support automated de-identification and normalization of SHI in clinical text, improving the scalability of information extraction from medical records while preserving patient privacy [23]. At the same time, the integration of LLMs with healthcare data introduces significant privacy and regulatory challenges, particularly when processing unstructured clinical documents that contain identifiable patient information. To address these concerns, prior work highlights the importance of privacy-preserving strategies such as de-identification pipelines, surrogate generation, and secure deployment environments to minimize the risk of re-identification while maintaining the analytical value of clinical datasets [24].

2.3 Process Flowchart

The objective of this study is to develop a program that transcribes doctor–patient voice recordings into verbatim text and extracts SHI. To improve extraction accuracy, both prompt design and post-processing procedures were refined. Figure 1 shows the overall processing workflow. First, the system inputs doctor–patient audio recordings and transcribes them into verbatim text. Next, word-level alignment is performed to accurately associate each word with its corresponding timestamp. Following alignment, SHI is extracted from the transcripts. Finally, the identified SHI is combined with the timestamp information and exported in a structured format.

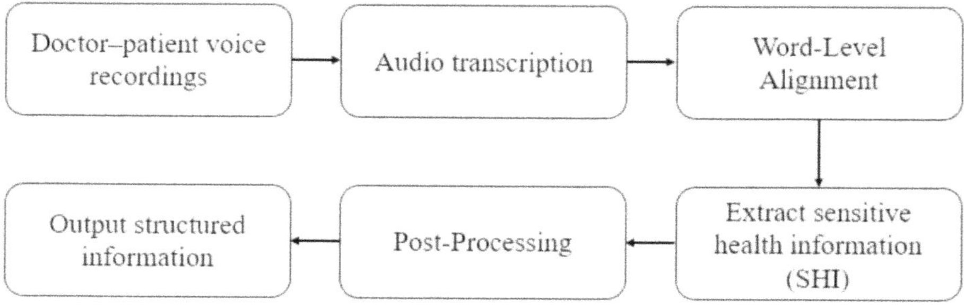

Fig. 1. SHI extraction workflow

2.4 Shi

The SHI categories adopted in this study are listed in Table 1.

Table 1. SHI categories [25]

SHI Category	SHI Type
Name	PATIENT / DOCTOR / USERNAME / FAMILYNAME / PERSONALNAME
Occupation	PROFESSION
Location	ROOM / DEPARTMENT / HOSPITAL / ORGANIZATION / STREET / CITY / DISTRICT / COUNTY / STATE / COUNTRY / ZIP / LOCATION-OTHER
Age	AGE
Date	DATE / TIME / DURATION / SET
Contact Information	PHONE / FAX / EMAIL / URL / IPADDRESS
Identifiers	SOCIAL_SECURITY_NUMBER / MEDICAL_RECORD_NUMBER / HEALTH_PLAN_NUMBER / ACCOUNT_NUMBER / LICENSE_NUMBER / VEHICLE_ID / DEVICE_ID / BIOMETRIC_ID / ID_NUMBER
Other	OTHER

2.5 Environment Setup

This study was implemented on Google Colab using a T4 GPU with 12.7 GB of system RAM and 15.0 GB of GPU memory. The pipeline employed pretrained models, including Whisper large-v3, WhisperX, and OpenAI GPT-4-Turbo, without the need for additional datasets.

2.6 Computation Methods and Model Architecture

This study employs Whisper, a transformer-based encoder–decoder model, to transcribe audio recordings into verbatim text. The multilingual capability of Whisper makes it suitable for our dataset, which contains both English and Chinese doctor–patient conversations. Its multiple model sizes allow flexible adaptation to different computational constraints. To maximize transcription accuracy, we adopt the large-v3 model, which contains approximately 1.55 billion parameters.

Although Whisper provides native timestamps, its word-level accuracy is limited. To overcome this issue, we incorporate WhisperX as the second pretrained model to perform word-level alignment. This step yields more precise timestamps, which are essential for accurate de-identification and downstream processing, especially when extracted entities are aligned with the original audio for precise SHI redaction.

For SHI extraction, we ultimately select OpenAI's GPT-4-Turbo. Although GPT-4.1 offers larger context capacity and higher potential resolution, it exhibits a greater tendency toward hallucination when handling long prompts and full audio transcripts. After comparative evaluation, GPT-4-Turbo was selected for its stability and consistency in structured extraction tasks. To enhance determinism and reproducibility, we set the generation parameters to temperature $= 0$ and top_p $= 0.1$, reducing randomness and improving classification reliability.

2.7 Training Procedure

Unlike conventional approaches that improve model performance through parameter fine-tuning, this study enhances model effectiveness via iterative prompt engineering and post-processing optimization. Instead of retraining models, we guide the pretrained OpenAI model to accurately extract SHI by providing precise, structured instructions.

We initially used the OpenAI API Playground to extract SHI from individual text samples. Through iterative testing and refinement, the prompt was gradually optimized until the extracted results closely matched the expected output. The finalized prompt was then integrated into a large-scale processing pipeline. Figure 2 shows a portion of the initial prompt; the full version included only basic task definitions, a brief list of SHI categories, and minimal formatting constraints.

```
#### Profession:
- "profession": Job titles or professions (e.g., "teacher", "nurse")
#### Location-related:
- "room": Room numbers (e.g., "Room 302")
- "department": Departments (e.g., "Cardiology")
- "hospital": Hospital names (e.g., "Taipei Veterans General Hospital")
- "organization": Non-hospital organizations (e.g., "WHO")
- "street": Streets or addresses (e.g., "123 Main St.")
- "city": Cities (e.g., "Taipei")
- "district": Districts (e.g., "Da'an District")
- "county": Counties (e.g., "Orange County")
- "state": States (e.g., "California")
- "country": Countries (e.g., "Taiwan")
- "zip": Postal or ZIP codes (e.g., "106")
- "location-other": Other location references (e.g., "building A")
#### Age and Time:
- "age":
Age or age range expressions.
Examples: "69-year-old", "in his 20s", "aged 15", "a teenager", "ages"

- "date":
Specific date expressions.
Examples: "2023-12-25", "May 10th", "last Friday", "yesterday", "this weekend", "now"
```

Fig. 2. Partial content of the first prompt version

To evaluate system performance, we used the DiffChecker platform to compare the model-generated transcripts and extracted SHI against ground-truth annotations. The color-coded visualization of DiffChecker facilitated the efficient identification of mismatches. The observed errors were classified into four primary categories:

1. **Inaccurate extraction:** Missing punctuation, incorrect capitalization, or inclusion of extraneous words.

2. **Misclassification:** Most frequently, confusion between family and personal names.
3. **Omission:** Sensitive information present in the transcript but not detected by the system.
4. **Over-identification:** Non-sensitive content incorrectly labeled as sensitive.

Based on these findings, we applied several prompt refinement strategies:

Reinforcing Rule Descriptions: Recurrent errors prompted the introduction of additional rules under a *CRITICAL RULE* section. A notable example involved confusion among the *time*, *duration*, and *set* categories in temporal expressions. Targeted rules and examples were added to resolve this issue (Fig. 3).

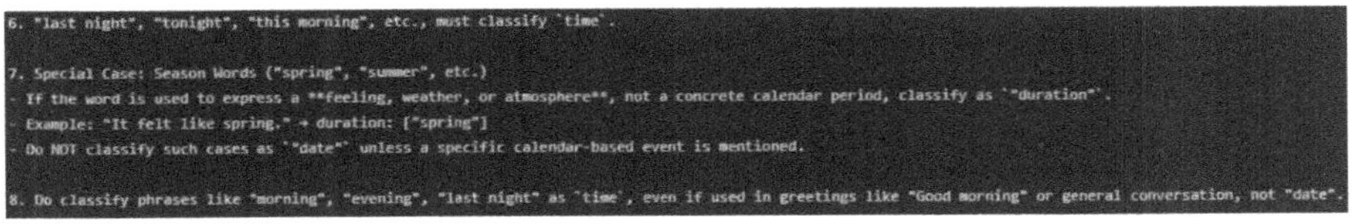

```
6. "last night", "tonight", "this morning", etc., must classify `time`.

7. Special Case: Season Words ("spring", "summer", etc.)
- If the word is used to express a **feeling, weather, or atmosphere**, not a concrete calendar period, classify as `"duration"`.
- Example: "It felt like spring." → duration: ["spring"]
- Do NOT classify such cases as `"date"` unless a specific calendar-based event is mentioned.

8. Do classify phrases like "morning", "evening", "last night" as `time`, even if used in greetings like "Good morning" or general conversation, not "date".
```

Fig. 3. Example of reinforcing rule descriptions

Expanding Examples and Rules: When misclassifications occurred, the prompt was supplemented with representative examples, both correct and incorrect, to clarify entity boundaries. For example, the phrase "Ivan's dad" was typically split into two individuals ("Ivan" and "Ivan's dad"), which was corrected by introducing explicit rules and examples (Fig. 4).

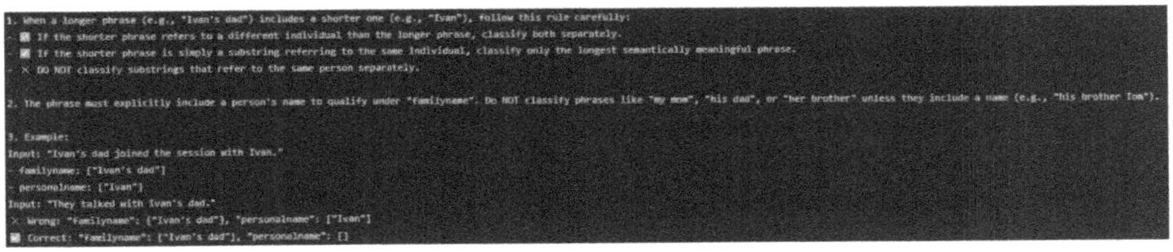

```
1. When a longer phrase (e.g., "Ivan's dad") includes a shorter one (e.g., "Ivan"), follow this rule carefully:
- ☑ If the shorter phrase refers to a different individual than the longer phrase, classify both separately.
- ☑ If the shorter phrase is simply a substring referring to the same individual, classify only the longest semantically meaningful phrase.
- ✗ DO NOT classify substrings that refer to the same person separately.

2. The phrase must explicitly include a person's name to qualify under "familyname". Do NOT classify phrases like "my mom", "his dad", or "her brother" unless they include a name (e.g., "his brother Tom").

3. Example:
Input: "Ivan's dad joined the session with Ivan."
- familyname: ["Ivan's dad"]
- personalname: ["Ivan"]
Input: "They talked with Ivan's dad."
✗ Wrong: "familyname": ["Ivan's dad"], "personalname": ["Ivan"]
☑ Correct: "familyname": ["Ivan's dad"], "personalname": []
```

Fig. 4. Example of expanding examples and rules

For discrepancies unrelated to extraction accuracy, such as formatting inconsistencies and extraneous tokens, a post-processing step was applied to ensure alignment with the reference annotations.

After each modification, 5–10 representative test cases were evaluated using either the main program or the OpenAI Playground to confirm that no new issues were introduced. After several rounds of refinement, a full evaluation was performed using the entire validation set, and the outputs were analyzed using DiffChecker to quantify improvements. Previously corrected cases were repeatedly retested to ensure that new edits did not reintroduce earlier errors. Finally, the updated system was submitted to the testing platform for precision-gain assessment.

3   Results

The audio recordings were transcribed into verbatim text, which was defined as Task 1. The evaluation of this task adopts word error rate (WER) and character error rate (CER), which are integrated to derive the mixed error rate (MER) as the overall performance indicator. As shown in Eq. 1, the MER is computed based on the following parameters: S, the total number of substitutions of Chinese characters and English words; D, the total number of deletions; I, the total number of insertions; N, the total number of characters and words in the reference transcript [25]. By jointly considering errors at both the word and character levels, the MER provides a more balanced and robust measure of transcription quality, mitigating the limitations associated with relying solely on either WER or CER.

$$\text{MER} = \frac{S + D + I}{N} \tag{1}$$

SHI identification is defined as Task 2, and its evaluation is performed using precision and recall, from which the macro F1-score is computed for each SHI category.

3.1   Task 1

The initial experiments were conducted using a validation set of approximately 1.4 GB, consisting entirely of English audio files. The performance scores are shown in Fig. 5. The scores fluctuated considerably during the first eight rounds of testing, with the highest and lowest MERs (0.2047 and 0.1029, respectively) occurring in the eighth and sixth rounds, respectively. From the ninth round onward, the results became more stable, with the worst MER being 0.0936 (in the tenth and eleventh rounds) and the best MER being 0.0942 (in the ninth round).

The instability in the earlier rounds was primarily due to the use of the Whisper large model during the first eight tests. Although this model shares the same number of parameters as Whisper large-v3, its transcription accuracy is markedly lower than that of Whisper large-v3. Although some variation in the MER is expected due to nondeterministic elements in processing, the magnitude of the observed fluctuations was unusually large and required further investigation.

Subsequent debugging revealed that the root cause was hallucination errors introduced by the OpenAI language model. Specifically, in the first eight rounds, Task 1 was performed by transcribing the audio into verbatim text using Whisper and then passing the transcripts to OpenAI to generate structured outputs. When hallucinations occurred, OpenAI returned inaccurate results, thereby inflating the MER scores.

To address this issue, we modified the pipeline to directly use the Whisper-generated transcripts as the final Task 1 output, thereby eliminating the OpenAI intermediate step. This change effectively prevented hallucination errors and resulted in more stable and reliable evaluation results.

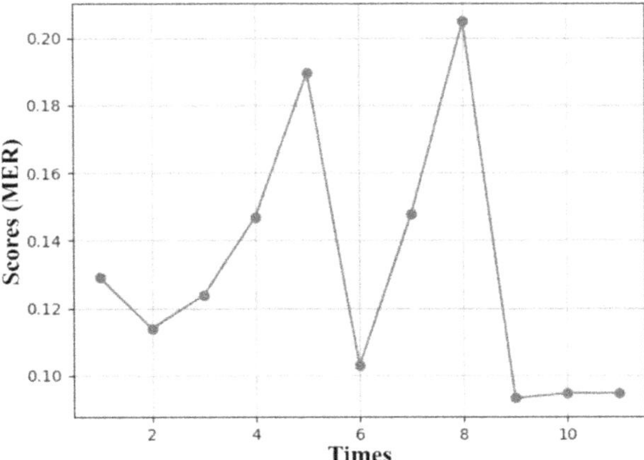

Fig. 5. Task 1 validation dataset scores

Then, we conducted testing using the 554.2 MB test set, which contained both Chinese and English audio recordings. The results are presented in Fig. 6. The Chinese and English audio files were processed separately. This decision was made because executing Chinese audio transcription led to system-level failures (Fig. 7), which required additional patching to resolve. Moreover, the transcriptions of Chinese audio were output in Simplified Chinese, necessitating a separate script to convert them into Traditional Chinese.

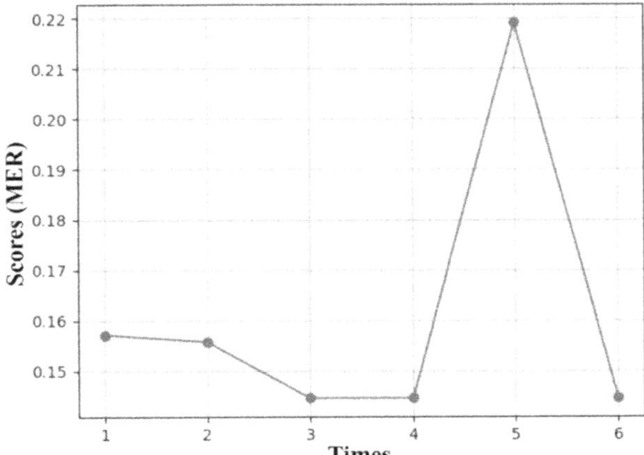

Fig. 6. Task 1 testing dataset scores

The worst performance (0.2191) was recorded in the fifth trial, where the output was generated directly from Whisper large-v3 without any post-processing. The overall score was lower than that of the validation set because Chinese audio transcription is inherently less accurate than English, particularly in the presence of background noise.

In subsequent trials, post-processing steps were applied, including filtering out English segments with translation mismatches and enriching Chinese transcripts with sentence segmentation and punctuation marks. These refinements improved performance, with the best score (0.1445) observed in the third, fourth, and sixth trials.

```
/usr/local/lib/python3.11/dist-packages/whisperx/alignment.py in get_wildcard_emission(frame_emission, tokens, blank_id)
    425
    426        # Get scores for non-wildcard positions
--> 427        regular_scores = frame_emission[tokens.clamp(min=0)]  # clamp to avoid -1 index
    428
    429        # Create a mask and compute the maximum value without modifying frame_emission

IndexError: tensors used as indices must be long, int, byte or bool tensors
```

Fig. 7. Example of system failure when processing Chinese audio without patching

3.2 Task 2

In the validation phase, OpenAI GPT-4.1 was employed to extract SHI. The evaluation results are summarized in Table 2. The "Number" column in the table represents the number of experimental runs.

Table 2. Task 2 validation dataset scores

Number	Precision	Recall	F1-Measure
#1	0.4878	0.5516	0.4832
#2	0.4824	0.5499	0.4794
#3	0.516	0.6182	0.5006
#4	0.5111	0.6404	0.5112
#5	0.5108	0.6373	0.5155
#6	0.5123	0.6421	0.5206
#7	0.5275	0.5977	0.5367
#8	0.5354	0.6019	0.5485
#9	0.5243	0.5844	0.5359
#10	0.5229	0.592	0.536
#11	0.5237	0.5927	0.5366

The prompt optimization process followed the previously described training methodology, and the post-processing involved three main functions:

1. Temporal alignment using WhisperX to obtain word-level timestamps, which were then matched with the SHI labels generated by GPT.
2. Standardization of formatting, including case normalization, punctuation removal, and time formatting.
3. Category-specific processing, where different SHI types were handled with the customized rules outlined in Table 3.

Table 3. Category-specific post-processing rules applied to different SHI types

Index	Description	Example
#1	Removes vague modifiers such as "around," "about," and "approximately."	about 30 years old → 30 years old
#2	Removes family relationship terms, retaining only the person's name.	Ivan's dad → Ivan
#3	Removes prefixes such as "Dr." and "dr."	Dr. Micah → Micah
#4	Removes common titles such as "Mr.," "Ms.," "Nurse," and "Prof."	Ms. Amy → Amy
#5	Removes suffixes indicating degrees or job titles such as "M.D.," "Ph.D.," and "R.N."	Amy Ph.D. → Amy
#6	Removes possessive forms such as 's, 's, and s'.	John's → John

During the initial testing phase on the test set, we employed OpenAI GPT-4.1 for SHI extraction. However, a significant number of hallucinated outputs were observed. After identifying this issue, we switched to GPT-4-Turbo for comparison and found that GPT-4.1 produced a considerably higher error rate. This discrepancy can be attributed to the combination of a long prompt (with many examples) and short verbatim transcripts derived from the test audio, which likely overwhelmed GPT-4.1. Nevertheless, some hallucinations were also observed in longer transcripts.

Table 4 presents the F1-measure scores across five rounds, showing an improvement from 0.4654 (Round 1) to 0.5147 (Rounds 5 and 6). To address the aforementioned challenges, the following three optimizations were implemented:

- **SHI Category-Specific Optimization**: Some SHI categories exhibited high recall but low precision, indicating over-prediction. As shown in Table 5, these categories typically exhibited low support. To improve the F1-measure, stricter rules were applied to these low-support categories to reduce false positives. These rules introduced additional filtering criteria and refined entity definitions. They limited the types of expressions considered valid entities, enforced stricter contextual checks, and excluded ambiguous or partial matches that previously contributed to false positives. This approach reduces over-prediction, thereby enhancing precision and the overall F1-measure.

- **Misclassification of Unsupported Categories**: Although categories such as USER-NAME, HEALTH_PLAN_NUMBER, ACCOUNT_NUMBER, LICENSE_NUMBER, VEHICLE_ID, DEVICE_ID, and BIOMETRIC_ID had zero true instances in the dataset, the model predicted them. We addressed this by deprioritizing these labels and guiding the model to prefer alternative, more likely classes within the same group.

- **Possessive Name Handling**: Named entities with possessive forms (e.g., "John's") were not captured during SHI recognition because GPT only returned the core name (e.g., "John"), whereas WhisperX aligned timestamps with the full possessive phrase (e.g., "John's"). To resolve this issue, we developed a custom module that searches for possessive names within the transcripts, resubmits those segments to OpenAI for secondary SHI recognition, and reconciles the results with timestamped data for final integration.

Table 4. Task 2 testing dataset scores

Number	Precision	Recall	F1-Measure
#1	0.4904	0.5696	0.4654
#2	0.5043	0.5611	0.4859
#3	0.5063	0.5669	0.4898
#4	0.5037	0.5868	0.5094
#5	0.5049	0.592	0.5147
#6	0.5049	0.592	0.5147

Table 5. SHI categories with high recall and low precision

SHI Type	Precision	Recall	F1-Measure	Support
PROFESSION	0.0469	0.9126	**0.0891**	2
ORGANIZATION	0.0985	0.7758	**0.1749**	6
PERSONALNAME	0.0151	0.4189	**0.0292**	4

4 Discussion

This study demonstrates that significant improvements in SHI identification can be achieved solely through prompt engineering, without the need to fine-tune model parameters. Unlike many models that require extensive training and substantial computational resources, the proposed approach lowers the technical barrier for implementation.

However, the use of OpenAI models in this study revealed hallucination issues. As noted in previous studies, "both closed as well as open-sourced Generative AI platforms had a common pitfall, that being hallucination" [26]. To mitigate its impact on SHI recognition performance, we selected a model with a lower-hallucination rate (Table 6). Although adopting a lower-hallucination model reduced the erroneous outputs, it also introduced a trade-off: decreased SHI identification accuracy. Within the context of this competition, improving SHI recognition accuracy was prioritized over minimizing hallucinations. This is because hallucinations are inherently less controllable, and their occurrence can only be reduced rather than completely eliminated. Moreover, repeated inference can still yield outputs without the presence of hallucinated content. Therefore, the primary objective of this study was to maximize SHI identification accuracy [26, 27].

The final optimized prompt was developed through multiple iterations. During this process, we observed instances in which predictions that were originally correct became incorrect after the optimized prompt was applied. Furthermore, the final prompt exhibited substantially lower recognition performance for Chinese than for English. This discrepancy can be attributed to two primary factors: first, the transcription of Chinese audio recordings contained more background noise than English recordings; second, the prompt still has scope for improvement in multilingual scenarios.

In addition, this study was limited to English and Chinese audio recordings. Nevertheless, Whisper supports nearly 100 languages, thereby providing significant potential for future expansion. However, transcription accuracy and alignment performance vary across languages, necessitating further testing and validation.

Table 6. Hallucination leaderboard [27]

Model	Hallucination Rate	Answer Rate
OpenAI GPT-4.1	2.0%	100.0%
OpenAI GPT-4-Turbo	1.7%	100.0%

5 Conclusion

This study successfully achieved and enhanced SHI identification using prompt engineering and post-processing techniques. During prompt design, four major issues were encountered: inaccurate extraction, misclassification, omission, and over-identification. To address these issues, we applied strategies such as reinforcing rule descriptions and expanding examples and prompt rules, which considerably improved model performance.

In addition, post-processing improved the SHI identification accuracy by correcting letter casing, removing unnecessary punctuation, formatting temporal expressions, and applying entity-specific refinement strategies based on SHI categories. By combining prompt optimization with tailored post-processing workflows, the overall SHI recognition performance was effectively improved.

Consequently, the proposed system achieved a ranking of 15th in Task 1, a ranking of sixth in Task 2, and an overall final ranking of 8th.

This study provides practical insights and methodoloFFgical guidance for addressing specific information-extraction challenges using prompt-based approaches and lightweight post-processing techniques.

Acknowledgments. The authors would like to express their sincere gratitude to Prof. Hong-Jie Dai from the Department of Electrical Engineering, National Kaohsiung University of Science and Technology (NKUST), for his kind consultations. Special thanks are also extended to Mr. Liang-Chun Fang, also from the Department of Electrical Engineering at NKUST, for his assistance with data organization and problem solving. Finally, the authors would like to thank the organizers of the AICUP Medical Speech Sensitive Information Recognition Challenge for providing the dataset and evaluation platform that supported the completion of this research.

Disclosure of Interests The authors have no competing interests to declare that are relevant to the content of this article.

References

1. Bannour, N., et al.: Privacy-preserving mimic models for clinical named entity recognition in French. J. Biomed. Inform. **130**, 1040731 (2022)
2. Zhuang, Y., et al.: MedNER: enhanced named entity recognition in medical corpus via optimized balanced and deep active learning. ACM Trans. Intell. Syst. Technol. **15**(5), 1–24 (2024)
3. Chen, Z., et al.: Meditron-70b: Scaling medical pretraining for large language models, 2023. URL https://arxiv. org/abs/2311.16079, (2023)
4. Sarker, A., et al.: Natural language processing for digital health in the era of large language models. Yearb. Med. Inform. **33**(01), 229–240 (2024)
5. Hu, Y., et al.: Improving large language models for clinical named entity recognition via prompt engineering. J. Am. Med. Inform. Assoc. **31**(9), 1812–1820 (2024)
6. Shyr, C., et al.: Identifying and extracting rare diseases and their phenotypes with large language models. J. Healthc. Inform. Res. **8**(2), 438–461 (2024)
7. Panchal, O., et al.: Benchmarking Large Language Models for De-Identification of Electronic Health Record Notes. 2026.
8. Kuhn, K., Kersken, V., Zimmermann, G.: Evaluating ASR confidence scores for automated error detection in user-assisted correction interfaces. In: Proceedings of the Extended Abstracts of the CHI Conference on Human Factors in Computing Systems (2025)
9. Le-Duc, K., et al.: Multimed: Multilingual medical speech recognition via attention encoder decoder. In: Proceedings of the 63rd Annual Meeting of the Association for Computational Linguistics (Volume 6: Industry Track) (2025)
10. Neuraz, A., et al.: TAXN: translate align extract normalize, a multilingual extraction tool for clinical texts. In: MedInfo 2023–the 19th World Congress on Medical and Health Informatics (2023)
11. Lien, C.-Y., et al.: Design of HL7 FHIR profiles for pathology reports integrated with pathology images. In: MEDINFO 2023—the Future Is Accessible, pp. 13–17. IOS Press (2024)
12. Bönisch, C., Kesztyüs, D., Kesztyüs, T.: FAIR+ R: making clinical data reliable through qualitative metadata. Stud. Health Technol. Inform. **310**(1), 99–103 (2024)
13. Neamatullah, I., et al.: Automated de-identification of free-text medical records. BMC Med. Inform. Decis. Mak. **8**(1), 32 (2008)
14. Ferrández, O., et al.: Evaluating current automatic de-identification methods with Veteran's health administration clinical documents. BMC Med. Res. Methodol. **12**(1), 109 (2012)
15. Dernoncourt, F., et al.: De-identification of patient notes with recurrent neural networks. J. Am. Med. Inform. Assoc. **24**(3), 596–606 (2017)
16. Aloqaily, A., et al.: Deep learning framework for advanced de-identification of protected health information. Future Internet. **17**(1), 47 (2025)
17. Cohn, I., et al.: Audio de-identification-a new entity recognition task. In: Proceedings of the 2019 Conference of the North American Chapter of the Association for Computational Linguistics: Human Language Technologies, Volume 2 (Industry Papers) (2019)
18. Berg, H., et al.: De-identification of clinical text for secondary use: research issues. Healthinf, 592–599 (2021)
19. Chen, A., et al.: Generation of surrogates for De-identification of electronic health records. Stud. Health Technol. Inform. **264**, 70–73 (2019)

20. Jonnagaddala, J., et al.: The OpenDeID corpus for patient de-identification. Sci. Rep. **11**(1), 19973 (2021)
21. Dai, H.J., et al.: Leveraging State-of-the-Art LLMs for the De-identification of Sensitive Health Information in Clinical Speech. medRxiv,: p. 2026.04.13.26349911 (2026).
22. Dai, H.J., et al.: A Clinical Speech Corpus with Temporally Aligned Sensitive Health Information (2026). https://www.medrxiv.org/content/10.64898/2026.03.31.26349906v2
23. Dai, H.-J., et al.: Leveraging large language models for the deidentification and temporal normalization of sensitive health information in electronic health records. npj Digit. Med. **8**(1), 517 (2025)
24. Jonnagaddala, J., Wong, Z.S.-Y.: Privacy preserving strategies for electronic health records in the era of large language models. npj Digit. Med. **8**(1), 34 (2025)
25. Codabench: https://www.codabench.org/competitions/4890/?secret_key=38d92718-cc4d-4907-9c65-c73419671268. https://www.codabench.org/competitions/4890/. Accessed 25 July 2025
26. Jayaram, M., et al.: Beyond automation: Ai-driven project management with openai and prompt engineering. In: 2024 International Conference on Electrical, Computer and Energy Technologies (ICECET), IEEE (2024).
27. Vectara: Hallucination Leaderboard, GitHub. https://github.com/vectara/hallucination-leaderboard. Accessed 25 July 2025

Named Entity Recognition in Chinese–English Speech Using Automatic Speech Recognition and Large Language Models

Lien-Hung Su[✉] [iD] and Jun-Sheng Lin [iD]

National Kaohsiung University of Science and Technology, Kaohsiung 807618, Taiwan
{F113154130,f113154131}@nkust.edu.tw

Abstract. This research proposes an automated sensitive health information (SHI) entity identification system for Chinese and English code-switched clinical speech. The framework first applies to the WhisperX model for local automatic speech recognition to generate transcripts with word-level timestamps. SHI entities are then identified using the LLaMA3-70B model via an application programming interface. A two-stage inference design leverages <think> tag chain-of-thought prompting to refine entity types and improve robustness on ambiguous mentions. Rule-based standardization and postprocessing include simplified-to-traditional conversion, spelling correction, duplicate truncation, regular-expression augmentation, and timestamp alignment, further enhancing output consistency. Experiments on the AI CUP 2025 task demonstrate that the framework achieves strong speech deidentification performance without task-specific model fine-tuning, offering a practical solution for privacy protection in bilingual medical data.

Keywords: Sensitive health information identification · Speech deidentification · Automatic speech recognition · large language model prompting · Chain-of-thought

1 Introduction

Sensitive health information (SHI) in spoken interactions is receiving increasing attention as speech-based applications expand across healthcare, virtual assistants, and customer support. In clinical conversations, SHI, such as patient names, ages, record numbers, and institutional identifiers, appear frequently, and improper handling of this information can violate privacy regulations.

Recent benchmarking studies [1] have compared leading LLMs including GPT-4, Gemini, and the LLaMA family on NER tasks across general and clinical domains, revealing that no single model dominates across all settings [2]. GPT-4 demonstrates strong performance on richly prompted clinical extraction tasks, Gemini shows advantages in few-shot entity classification, and open-source LLaMA models offer competitive reasoning capability with greater deployment flexibility. Crucially, performance across all models remains highly sensitive to prompt design rather than raw model

J. Jonnagaddala et al. (Eds.): IW-DMRN 2025, CCIS 2908, pp. 44–58, 2026.
https://doi.org/10.1007/978-981-92-2282-7_4

scale alone. This landscape motivates the present study's adoption of LLaMA3-70B as a practical balance between reasoning capacity, open accessibility, and suitability for API-based deployment in privacy-sensitive clinical environments where proprietary model constraints may limit adoption.

Secondary use of electronic health records (EHRs) holds significant promise for enhancing clinical outcomes and advancing personalized medicine; however, it simultaneously raises serious concerns regarding the exposure of sensitive health information (SHI). Compounding this challenge, inconsistent temporal formats across clinical narratives hinder accurate interpretation, making both de-identification and temporal normalization essential preprocessing steps for safe secondary data use. To advance research in this space, the SREDH/AI CUP 2023 competition examined the application of LLMs to these tasks using 3,244 pathology reports with surrogated SHIs and normalized dates, drawing 291 competing teams. Results presented at the IW-DMRN workshop in 2024 showed that top-performing teams achieved macro-F1 scores exceeding 0.8, with 77.2% of participants employing LLMs which underscored their growing centrality in clinical NLP [3]. Comparative analysis of competition results against in-context learning and fine-tuned LLMs revealed that fine-tuning, particularly with lower-rank adaptation, boosts performance but plateaus or degrades in models exceeding 6B parameters due to overfitting. These findings collectively highlight the value of data augmentation, strategic training design, and hybrid approaches, while emphasizing that effective LLM-based de-identification must balance performance with the legal and ethical demands of regulated healthcare environments, ensuring both privacy preservation and model interpretability.

Most existing deidentification research focuses on written or structured records. Neamatullah et al. [4] demonstrated effective text-based deidentification, while Cohn et al. [5] highlighted that speech deidentification is substantially more challenging due to transcription noise, speaker variability, and the need for temporal localization. Conventional speech-based methods often depend on large, labeled datasets and domain-specific models, making deployment costly and less portable. These challenges are further amplified in Chinese English code-switched speech, where mixed-language structure, spoken-style variation, simplified–traditional script mismatches, and speech-recognition errors complicate reliable SHI detection.

To address this gap, we propose a two-stage framework that combines WhisperX transcription with LLaMA3-70B prompting for SHI entity identification. The system performs transcription, SHI extraction, label refinement, and rule-based postprocessing without requiring task-specific fine-tuning. In addition, we investigate chain-of-thought (CoT) prompting as an auxiliary refinement step for a small subset of ambiguous cases.

The primary contributions of this study are as follows:

1. **Two-stage prompting architecture.** We introduce a two-stage LLaMA3-70B prompting approach for SHI identification in Chinese English code-switched clinical speech, enabling direct processing of transcripts without fine-tuning.
2. **Transcript standardization and postprocessing.** We implement complementary transcript-standardization and SHI postprocessing modules that combine rule-based normalization and regular expressions with LLaMA3-70B predictions, resulting in substantial improvements in end-to-end performance.

3. **Comprehensive evaluation.** We conduct an extensive evaluation of the proposed framework on the AI CUP 2025 task, including ablation studies and automatic speech recognition (ASR) error analysis, to demonstrate its effectiveness.

Notably, the proposed system ranked third in Task 2 (entity identification) of the AI CUP 2025 Medical Speech Deidentification Challenge. The remainder of this paper is organized as follows. Section 2 reviews related work, and Sect. 3 presents the proposed framework. Section 4 reports the experimental setup and results. Section 5 concludes the paper and outlines future research directions.

1.1 Related Work

Speech deidentification is commonly studied at two levels: text-level methods, which extract SHI from transcripts, and audio-level methods, which additionally require speech recognition, entity localization, and timestamp alignment. The latter is generally more challenging because extraction performance is tightly coupled to transcription quality.

Early text-level systems were primarily rule-based. Neamatullah et al. [4] employed handcrafted templates and regular expressions to remove Sensitive health information (SHI) from clinical text; however, such approaches are brittle when applied to noisy speech transcripts. Cohn et al. [5] later framed audio deidentification as an end-to-end task and showed that speech-recognition errors and semantic ambiguity substantially affect SHI localization.

The secondary use of EHRs with LLMs, introduces significant privacy challenges that extend beyond technical performance considerations [6]. National and international regulatory frameworks such as GDPR and HIPAA provide foundational protections, yet they do not prescribe specific mitigation strategies for the risks introduced by generative AI systems. Effective risk reduction requires a combination of targeted approaches, including privacy-preserving locally deployed LLMs, synthetic data generation, differential privacy, and systematic de-identification. The appropriate selection and combination of these strategies depend on the nature of the downstream task, and must be carefully calibrated to ensure compliance with patient privacy regulations while preserving the utility of the clinical data. This tension between model capability and regulatory compliance remains a central consideration in the design of any LLM-based clinical NLP system.

Recent advances in multilingual speech recognition, such as Whisper [7], have improved transcript quality for Chinese–English code-switched speech, although normalization remains necessary for clinical applications. In parallel, large language models (LLMs) have demonstrated the ability to perform SHI identification via prompting without task-specific training [8], and CoT prompting has been shown to enhance type reasoning under ambiguity [9].

However, despite these developments, Chinese English code-switched clinical speech deidentification remains underexplored. To address this gap, we propose a two-stage LLaMA3-70B prompting framework applied to WhisperX transcripts, augmented with rule-based standardization and postprocessing.

2 Methods

2.1 Dataset

The experiments were conducted using the SREDH-AICup SHI speech corpus 2025 which is constructed using OpenDeID corpus v2 dataset, which is released by SREDH consortium [10, 11]. The datasets provided were translated to Chinese and used for the AI CUP 2025, Chinese–English medical speech de-identification task [12]. These datasets comprise speech recordings, organizer-supplied transcripts, and manually annotated sensitive health information (SHI) entities with corresponding timestamp metadata, enabling evaluation of both automatic speech recognition accuracy and time-aligned entity identification. The training split contains complete transcripts with entity labels to support model selection and development, while the validation split serves as the primary benchmark for SHI recognition performance [13]. No external corpora or additional segmentation were introduced, ensuring that all results reflect performance on the standardized competition data.

2.2 System Overview

We propose a modular speech deidentification system for Chinese English code-switched doctor–patient conversations. As shown in Fig. 1, the framework integrates WhisperX transcription, a two-stage LLaMA3-70B SHI identification module, and rule-based postprocessing to generate structured, time-aligned outputs.

Given a WAV audio recording, WhisperX first produces a transcript with word-level timestamps. The transcript is then standardized through simplified-to-traditional conversion, spelling correction, and duplicate truncation. The cleaned text is processed in two stages using LLaMA3-70B: the first stage extracts and labels candidate sensitive entities, and the second stage uses CoT prompting to refine uncertain or ambiguous labels. A final postprocessing module applies regular-expression and keyword rules, restores timestamps, and orders entities chronologically, yielding a deidentified transcript with time-aligned entity spans. The system is implemented in Python (Jupyter Notebook), with WhisperX running locally and LLaMA3-70B accessed via an application programming interface (API).

2.3 ASR Module

In the proposed framework, WhisperX is used for speech transcription. WhisperX extends the OpenAI Whisper model with multilingual recognition and word-level alignment, making it suitable for Chinese–English code-switched clinical recordings. The model runs locally on WAV inputs and produces time-aligned transcripts for subsequent SHI annotation.

To mitigate transcription noise in the AI CUP 2025 data, we apply a post-decoding standardization step. This step converts simplified Chinese to traditional Chinese, corrects frequent spelling and tokenization errors, and removes duplicated segments before sensitive-entity identification.

Fig. 1. Overview of the proposed Chinese–English speech de-identification pipeline.

We evaluated multiple WhisperX model sizes on the official AI CUP 2025 training set, using character error rate (CER), word error rate (WER), and mixed error rate (MER). Larger models generally improved CER and MER, with the large-v3 model achieving the best overall MER; therefore, this model was adopted for all experiments.

2.4 Named Entity Recognition Module

In the proposed framework, sensitive-entity identification is carried out using a two-stage LLM architecture. The first stage extracts candidate entities, and the second stage refines their types.

Conventional sequence-labeling methods, such as conditional random fields (CRFs) and bidirectional long short-term memory CRF (BiLSTM-CRF) models [14], perform well on clean text but are less robust on speech transcripts that contain Chinese–English code-switching and transcription noise. These methods also require substantial feature engineering and large labeled datasets. In contrast, LLMs can be applied directly through prompting, leveraging their contextual reasoning to process unstructured, bilingual transcripts without task-specific training.

Stage 1: Entity Extraction and Preliminary Classification

In the first stage, the LLM performs initial sensitive-entity extraction and type assignment from the speech transcript. The prompt specifies the predefined SHI categories and their definitions (Table 1) and provides few-shot examples to clarify the semantic scope and output format (Table 2).

Because this stage operates on noisy, code-switched transcripts, the model may still generate type errors or boundary inconsistencies. Therefore, the preliminary outputs are forwarded to the second stage for semantic verification and label refinement.

Stage 2: Category Refinement and Semantic Reasoning

In the second stage, the LLM refines the labels produced in the first stage. We employ CoT prompting to guide semantic verification and type correction, reducing errors arising

Table 1. SHI category definitions used for model prompting and evaluation.

Category	Description
Date	Extract when the expression refers to a specific calendar point, named date, or time-referenced event. Examples: "now," "on Friday," "Monday," "August 5," "May," "last year," "next week," "today," "yesterday," "tomorrow," "Christmas," "New Year's Eve"

Table 2. Few-shot prompt examples to illustrate the SHI categories and required input–output format for prompting in the first stage.

Sentence	Expected Output
Dr. **Connie** examined patient **Florrie Minion** at **Kangaroo Island Health Service** on **June 20, 1989**. Her medical record number **4402074.WNE** and lab ID **44B20748** were recorded in the **Department of Cardiology**, located at **Blue Cow Street**, **Camden Haven**, **Western Australia**, ZIP **5067**.	**DOCTOR**: Connie **PATIENT**: Florrie Minion **HOSPITAL**: Kangaroo Island Health Service **DATE**: June 20, 1989 **MEDICAL_RECORD_NUMBER**: 4402074.WNE **ID_NUMBER**: 44B20748 **DEPARTMENT**: Department of Cardiology **STREET**: Blue Cow Street **CITY**: Camden Haven **STATE**: Western Australia **ZIP**: 5067

from ambiguous references and unclear boundaries. The prompt incorporates key annotation rules and counterexamples to distinguish closely related categories, such as HOSPITAL versus ORGANIZATION, thereby improving label consistency in challenging cases.

For example, "Friday morning" should be labeled TIME, and "3HR State Surgical Unit" should be labeled DEPARTMENT rather than HOSPITAL or ORGANIZATION. To support such disambiguation, the refined category criteria are summarized in Table 3, and representative CoT prompt examples are shown in Table 4.

Table 3. Refined SHI category criteria used in the second stage for type disambiguation.

Category	Description
Date	Refers to a full day or longer period (e.g., today, tomorrow, this week, or August 21)

In the two-stage design, the first-stage model processes the transcript to produce candidate sensitive-entity spans with preliminary labels. The second-stage model then reviews the transcript together with these predictions and uses CoT prompting to verify and refine the labels in ambiguous cases.

Table 4. CoT prompt examples used in the second stage to refine first-stage SHI labels.

Classification	Model Output
TIME: this morning	<think>"this morning" is a time span within the day, so it should be TIME

2.5 Postprocessing and Integration Module

To improve the completeness and usability of the sensitive-entity identification outputs, we apply a postprocessing and integration module after the LLM predictions. This module corrects labeling errors, recovers missed entities when possible, and aligns all entities with their corresponding timestamps.

The postprocessing strategy comprises the following components:

1. **Format checking and cleaning.** Invalid or malformed predictions are removed to ensure a consistent output structure.
2. **Regex-based augmentation and label correction.** Regular expressions and category-mapping rules are used to recover commonly missed types and resolve frequent label confusions.
3. **Chinese-specific enhancement and synonym mapping.** Lexicon-based mappings address traditional–simplified variation and other Chinese-specific surface forms.
4. **Timestamp alignment.** Entity spans are mapped to the ASR word-level timestamps, with safeguards to handle boundary shifts caused by transcription noise.
5. **Entity ordering and consistency integration.** Entities are merged and deduplicated when necessary, then sorted by file and time to produce a coherent final output.

To clarify the purpose, design principles, and application scenarios for each strategy, Table 5 summarizes the specific implementation methods and their corresponding use cases.

Table 5. Summary of rule-based postprocessing techniques to refine and normalize the sensitive-entity identification outputs, including format filtering, regex-based augmentation, label conversion, entity recovery, and timestamp-based ordering.

Type	Description	Examples
Invalid Line Removal	Removes any line that is malformed or contains no entity, preventing downstream errors.	The line "27688 HOSPITAL" contains only a category with no entity and is therefore discarded.
Regular Expression	Uses regular-expression patterns to extract fixed-format items.	Directly captures "Dr. V. Winant" and labels it as DOCTOR.

(continued)

Table 5. (continued)

Type	Description	Examples
Keyword-based Conversion	Applies predefined semantic rules and keyword lists to force-convert labels. Handles: **Time** categories (TIME / DATE / DURATION / SET) **Organization** categories (HOSPITAL / DEPARTMENT)	"3HR State Surgical Unit" is relabeled **DEPARTMENT** (was ORGANIZATION). "Monday morning" is relabeled **TIME** (was DATE). "today" is relabeled **DATE** (was TIME).
JSON-based Extraction	Looks up entities in an entity-to-category dictionary (JSON) built from the training/validation sets, automatically adding missing labels and avoiding false negatives.	If the JSON file contains **today**, every occurrence of today in the test data is automatically labeled DATE.
Timestamp Insertion	Inserts the ASR-generated timestamps for each entity span.	DATE today → DATE 16.332 16.613 today
Output Sorting	After aggregation, entities are sorted by file ID and start time; rules merge duplicates and overlapping spans to ensure consistent structure.	315DURATION7.967 9.06915 min 315TIME9.3299.65morning

3 Results

3.1 Experimental Setup

The dataset used in our experiments were taken from the official AI CUP 2025 training and validation sets. These datasets contain speech recordings, organizer-provided transcripts, and manual sensitive-entity annotations. Only the official data were used for system development and evaluation, with no additional segmentation or external corpora.

The training set includes complete Mandarin transcripts with entity labels, enabling speech-recognition model selection. The validation set provides entity labels with timestamp metadata and serves as the official evaluation split for sensitive-entity identification (Task 2). Accordingly, Task 2 results are reported on the validation set, while speech recognition (Task 1) is evaluated on the training set using CER, WER, and MER.

In our experimental evaluation, we compared WhisperX models of different sizes (tiny, base, small, medium, and large-v3) on the training set using these error metrics. The corresponding results are summarized in Table 6.

Table 6. Performance of WhisperX model variants on training set.

Model Variant	CER	WER	MER
tiny	0.0974	0.2212	0.1584
base	0.0874	0.2115	0.1366
small	0.0770	0.1927	0.1177
medium	0.0753	**0.1893**	0.1107
large-v3	**0.0747**	0.1905	**0.1067**

CER, WER, and MER are computed through direct string comparison with the reference transcripts. No text normalization (e.g., number conversion, punctuation standardization, or full-width/half-width conversion) is applied. Consequently, semantically equivalent outputs may still be penalized for minor formatting differences. For example, producing "3" instead of the reference "三" increases the CER and MER despite no change in meaning.

All speech-recognition, standardization, and analysis modules were executed locally on a Windows 11 Pro (64-bit) desktop equipped with an NVIDIA GeForce RTX 4070 SUPER GPU (12 GB VRAM), 32 GB RAM, and a 13th-generation Intel Core i7–13700 CPU. Sensitive-entity identification was performed via the Groq cloud API using the LLaMA3-70B model.

3.2 Output Correction and Postprocessing

WhisperX transcripts often contain noise, such as simplified Chinese characters, spelling errors, and duplicated segments. Using these raw transcripts directly for sensitive-entity identification can cause boundary errors and type confusion, reducing overall reliability. To address this, we apply postprocessing to enhance transcript quality and enforce a consistent structure before downstream identification.

The postprocessing strategy focuses on three key aspects:

1. **Simplified-to-Traditional Conversion.** WhisperX may output simplified Chinese. We automatically convert these characters to traditional Chinese to match the annotation standard and reduce form-based mismatches during sensitive-entity identification.
2. **Spelling Correction.** A lightweight correction step is applied to fix frequent recognition errors and misspellings, based on common lexical patterns observed in the ASR outputs.
3. **Duplicate Output Truncation.** Long recordings may contain repeated phrases produced by the recognizer. These duplicated segments are detected and removed to improve transcript conciseness and readability.

These postprocessing steps are applied immediately after speech transcription and before sensitive-entity identification. Table 7 presents representative examples of simplified-to-traditional conversion, spelling correction, and duplicate truncation. Collectively, these refinements produce cleaner transcripts and provide more reliable inputs for downstream identification.

Table 7. Examples of ASR output issues and corresponding corrected results.

Type	Original Sentence	Corrected Sentence
Simplified-to-traditional Conversion	急诊的但是现在脑压太高不能开刀主任说先送ICU为什么不先留在你们观察室呢开刀房马上就送来两个没有床位啦阿长你要不要去急诊室看一看旅行团吃宵夜中毒的全满了好了好了就送到旁边去	急診的但是現在腦壓太高不能開刀主任說先送ICU爲什麼不先留在你們觀察室呢開刀房馬上就送來兩個沒有牀位啦阿長你要不要去急診室看一看旅行團喫宵夜中毒的全滿了好了好了就送到旁邊去
Spelling Correction	急診的但是現在腦壓太高不能開刀主任說先送ICU爲什麼不先留在你們觀察室呢開刀房馬上就送來兩個沒有牀位啦阿長你要不要去急診室看一看旅行團喫宵夜中毒的全滿了好了好了就送到旁邊去	急診的但是現在腦壓太高不能開刀主任說先送ICU爲什麼不先留在你們觀察室呢開刀房馬上就送來兩個沒有床位啦阿長你要不要去急診室看一看旅行團吃宵夜中毒的全滿了好了好了就送到旁邊去
Duplicate Output Truncation	真的OK好…來, 進手術房, 快點快…來, 走了阿翔…快點…阿翔…阿翔…阿翔…阿翔…阿翔…阿翔…阿翔…阿翔…阿翔…阿翔…阿翔…阿翔…阿翔…阿翔…	真的OK好…來, 進手術房, 快點快…來, 走了阿翔…快點…阿翔…阿翔…阿翔…阿翔…阿翔…

To assess the impact of the postprocessing modules—specifically simplified-to-traditional conversion, spelling correction, and duplicate output truncation—on speech recognition quality, we applied the full postprocessing workflow to outputs from the WhisperX large-v3 model. CER, WER, and MER were then recalculated.

The comparison showed improvements across all metrics, although the magnitude of improvement varied.

These results indicate that the postprocessing modules enhanced transcription quality, which in turn contributed to stronger performance in downstream NER tasks. A detailed breakdown of metric changes is provided in Table 8.

Table 8. Improvements in CER, WER, and MER after postprocessing using the WhisperX large-v3 model

Model	Processing Status	CER	WER	MER
large-v3	Original Output	0.0747	0.1905	0.1067
large-v3	Post-processed Output	**0.0722**	0.1905	**0.0957**

3.3 SHI Identification Ablation Study

To evaluate the contribution of the rule-based postprocessing module, we compared three NER configurations on the validation set: (1) LLM-only, where named entities are extracted and classified solely by the two-stage LLaMA3-70B module without rule-based refinement; (2) rule-only, where handcrafted rules—including regular expressions and keyword-based mappings—are directly applied to the transcripts without using LLM outputs; and (3) hybrid (LLM + rule-based), where LLM predictions are subsequently refined by the rule-based module for category correction, augmentation, and filtering.

Table 9 summarizes the overall F1-scores of the three configurations. The LLM-only system achieved an F1-score of 0.5467, reflecting reasonable coverage but limited robustness to transcription noise and inconsistent formatting. The rule-only system attained a lower F1-score of 0.4122; while precise for patterns matching predefined rules, it lacks contextual understanding and fails to recognize entities outside fixed formats. In contrast, the hybrid configuration achieved an F1-score of 0.7226, substantially outperforming both standalone approaches and demonstrating the advantage of combining LLM predictions with deterministic rule-based corrections.

Figure 2 breaks down F1-scores by entity type for several representative categories—FAMILYNAME, ORGANIZATION, DATE, and SET—across the three configurations. For FAMILYNAME and ORGANIZATION, the rule-only system achieved the highest F1-scores. In these categories, deterministic patterns are relatively reliable, whereas LLM-based predictions tend to introduce false positives, reducing precision and F1. For DATE, the LLM-only and hybrid configurations achieved similarly high F1-scores, while the rule-only system performed poorly, indicating that contextual understanding beyond simple patterns is necessary. For SET, the hybrid system clearly outperformed both baselines, demonstrating that LLM predictions and rule-based normalization complement each other when both semantic interpretation and format regularization are required.

The results indicate that combining the LLaMA3-70B model with rule-based postprocessing effectively leverages the complementary strengths of semantic modeling and deterministic normalization. The rule-based module improves precision on structured entity types, while the LLM provides broader coverage for ambiguous and code-switched mentions. This ablation study clearly demonstrates the importance of the proposed postprocessing strategies for end-to-end SHI identification.

Table 9. Performance comparison of different NER module combinations (F1-score).

Method	Description	F1-score
LLM-only	Uses only LLaMA3 output without rule-based postprocessing	0.5467
Rule-only	Applies regular expressions and JSON-based lookup rules only	0.4122
LLM + Rule (Hybrid)	Combines LLaMA3 output with rule-based corrections and augmentation	**0.7226**

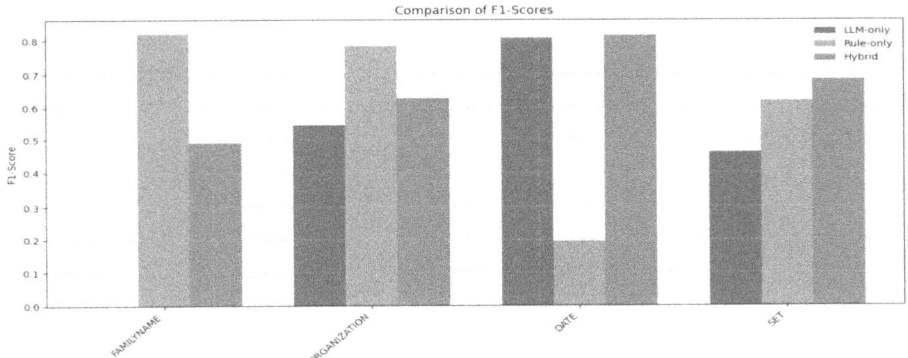

Fig. 2. Comparison of F1-scores for three NER configurations (LLM-only, Rule-only, and Hybrid) across representative entity types.

This three-way comparison quantifies the contribution of the rule-based postprocessing module.

3.4 Qualitative Analysis of CoT Prompting

To evaluate the contribution of CoT prompting with the <think> tag in the second stage, we examined cases where the second-stage LLaMA3-70B model revised first-stage labels. Only a small number of entities were affected, and the changes included both beneficial refinements and clear errors, suggesting that CoT serves as a lightweight complement rather than a primary driver of performance.

For example, a helpful change involved the phrase "SWAMP's department," initially labeled as ORGANIZATION in the first stage. The CoT-enabled second stage revised it to DEPARTMENT, correctly reflecting a department-level unit. Conversely, a harmful change occurred with "tomorrow hospital," initially labeled HOSPITAL; the second stage incorrectly reassigned it to DATE, likely overemphasizing the temporal cue "tomorrow." These examples indicate that organization- and location-related mentions in conversational transcripts are particularly prone to type confusion when strong contextual cues overlap with entity boundaries.

Overall, CoT prompting can correct some difficult labels but may also introduce false positive or type errors. Given its limited interventions and mixed effects, CoT should be regarded as a minor refinement step rather than a primary contributor to the overall SHI identification performance of the proposed framework.

3.5 Impact of ASR Errors on Sensitive-Entity Identification Performance

To assess the impact of transcription quality on downstream sensitive-entity identification, we evaluated the same pipeline using two transcript sources: organizer-provided human transcripts and WhisperX large-v3 transcripts. All other components and settings were identical; only the transcript source differed.

As shown in Table 10, the human-transcript condition achieved precision, recall, and F1-score of 0.7883, 0.7383, and 0.7501, respectively. Using WhisperX transcripts reduced precision to 0.7358, while recall remained comparable at 0.7341, resulting in an F1-score of 0.7226—an absolute drop of approximately 0.028. These results indicate that transcription errors primarily reduce precision due to boundary shifts or partial matches, while recall is less affected.

Table 10. SHI identification results using human-annotated vs. WhisperX transcripts.

Transcript Source	Precision	Recall	F1-score
Human-annotated	0.7883	0.7383	0.7501
WhisperX large-v3	0.7358	0.7341	0.7226

4 Discussion

4.1 Summary of Experimental Observations

This study presents a modular speech deidentification framework that combines WhisperX transcription with a two-stage LLaMA3-70B sensitive-entity identification module and rule-based postprocessing. Experimental results demonstrate that integrating LLM predictions with deterministic refinement achieves reliable performance on Chinese–English code-switched speech without task-specific fine-tuning.

The framework delivers strong accuracy while maintaining consistency and interpretability in entity extraction, highlighting its practical potential for real-world Chinese–English speech processing applications.

4.2 Limitations and Practical Considerations

The proposed framework relies on the LLaMA3-70B model, accessed via an external API, which introduces practical constraints. First, latency and usage costs can be significant in large-scale deployment, as each transcript requires two model passes.

Second, cloud-based models raise privacy and compliance concerns for clinical data, necessitating secure handling or, where feasible, on-premises or privacy-preserving deployments.

Additionally, end-to-end performance remains sensitive to transcription quality, as shown by the drop in sensitive-entity identification scores when automatic transcripts replace human transcripts. Future work will explore lightweight local models, privacy-aware LLM deployments, and noise-robust strategies to mitigate transcription-induced errors.

A critical yet often understated component of clinical de-identification pipelines is the generation of realistic surrogates to replace identified SHI [15]. As highlighted in prior work, unstructured EHRs represent invaluable research resources, but protected health information must be systematically removed before such records can be shared. The de-identification process involves two core steps: accurately identifying sensitive entities within the document and replacing them with plausible surrogate values that preserve the linguistic and structural realism of the original record. This surrogate replacement strategy is preferable to simple redaction, as blanket removal of sensitive spans can distort clinical context and reduce the utility of de-identified records for downstream research tasks. Automated surrogate generation algorithms, such as those demonstrated on Health Science Alliance corpora developed specifically for de-identification system development, offer a scalable path toward producing realistic synthetic replacements that maintain document coherence. In the context of the present framework, surrogate quality directly influences both the fidelity of training data and the robustness of evaluation, as models trained or tested on poorly surrogated records may learn artifacts of the replacement process rather than genuine SHI patterns. Future iterations of this system should therefore consider integrating a dedicated surrogate generation module to complement the de-identification pipeline and produce outputs suitable for open research sharing.

5   Conclusion

This paper presents an end-to-end speech deidentification framework for the AI CUP 2025 Chinese English code-switched clinical speech task. The pipeline integrates WhisperX transcription, a two-stage LLaMA3-70B sensitive-entity identification module, and rule-based postprocessing, enabling robust handling of code-switching, transcription noise, and varied SHI expressions.

Experimental results validate the framework's effectiveness. The hybrid configuration substantially outperformed LLM-only and rule-only approaches (F1-scores: 0.7226 vs. 0.5467 and 0.4122), highlighting the value of deterministic refinement. Performance also decreased when using automatic transcripts instead of human transcripts (F1-score: 0.7226 vs. 0.7501), demonstrating sensitivity to transcription quality. CoT prompting provides a lightweight second-stage refinement that corrects a small subset of challenging cases but is not the primary driver of overall performance.

Overall, the proposed framework delivers a competitive and reproducible solution for SHI identification in bilingual clinical speech and serves as a practical reference for privacy protection in multilingual healthcare settings.

Future research may focus on enhancing ASR robustness for noisy and code-switched clinical speech, as transcription errors remain a key bottleneck for end-to-end SHI identification. Another direction is the development of more advanced prompting or self-refinement strategies to better address ambiguous or context-dependent SHI mentions. Extending the framework to additional languages or medical domains, and exploring domain adaptation without requiring large, labeled datasets, also represent promising avenues for improving generalizability and practical deployment in multilingual healthcare environments.

Acknowledgments. The authors thank the organizers of the AI CUP 2025 competition for providing the official SREDH-AICup SHI speech corpus 2025 and evaluation platform, which served as the foundation for this research.

Disclosure of Interests. The authors declare no competing interests relevant to the content of this article.

References

1. Panchal, O., et al., Benchmarking Large Language Models for De-Identification of Electronic Health Record Notes. 2026.
2. Dai, H.-J., et al.: Leveraging state-of-the-art llms for the de-identification of sensitive health information in clinical speech. medRxiv. p. 2026.04.13.26349911 (2026)
3. Dai, H.-J., et al.: Leveraging large language models for the deidentification and temporal normalization of sensitive health information in electronic health records. npj Digit. Med. **8**(1), 517 (2025)
4. Neamatullah, I., et al.: Automated de-identification of free-text medical records. BMC Med. Inform. Decis. Mak. **8**(1), 32 (2008)
5. Cohn, I., et al.: Audio de-identification-a new entity recognition task. In: Proceedings of the 2019 Conference of the North American Chapter of the Association for Computational Linguistics: Human Language Technologies, vol. 2 (Industry Papers) (2019)
6. Jonnagaddala, J., Wong, Z.S.-Y.: Privacy preserving strategies for electronic health records in the era of large language models. npj Digit. Med. **8**(1), 34 (2025)
7. Radford, A., et al.: Robust speech recognition via large-scale weak supervision. In: International Conference on Machine Learning. PMLR (2023)
8. Brown, T., et al.: Language models are few-shot learners. Adv. Neural Inf. Proces. Syst. **33**, 1877–1901 (2020)
9. Wei, J., et al.: Chain-of-thought prompting elicits reasoning in large language models. Adv. Neural Inf. Proces. Syst. **35**, 24824–24837 (2022)
10. Jonnagaddala, J., et al.: The OpenDeID corpus for patient de-identification. Sci. Rep. **11**(1), 19973 (2021)
11. SREDH: SREDH Consortium (2025). Available from: https://www.sredhconsortium.org/.
12. Dai, H., et al.: Leveraging State-of-the-Art LLMs for the De-Identification of Sensitive Health Information in Clinical Speech (2026)
13. Dai, H.J., et al.: A Clinical Speech Corpus with Temporally Aligned Sensitive Health Information (2026). https://www.medrxiv.org/content/10.64898/2026.03.31.26349906v2
14. Lample, G., et al.: Neural architectures for named entity recognition. In: Proceedings of the 2016 Conference of the North American Chapter of the Association for Computational Linguistics: Human Language Technologies (2016)
15. Chen, A., et al.: Generation of surrogates for De-identification of electronic health records. Stud. Health Technol. Inform. **264**, 70–73 (2019)

A Two-Stage Generative Framework
for Sensitive Health Information Extraction
and Temporal Normalization in Medical Records

Ping-Hsien Lin[1]([✉]) [iD], Pratham Nandy[2] [iD], and Chen-Yu Wen[1] [iD]

[1] Department of Electrical Engineering, National Kaohsiung University of Science and Technology, Kaohsiung, Taiwan
{C111154209,C111154215}@nkust.edu.tw
[2] CGD Health Pvt. Ltd., Mumbai, India
pratham@cgdealth.com

Abstract. This study evaluates the performance of automatic speech recognition and sensitive personal information extraction models in medical speech, with a particular focus on improving the accuracy of sensitive health in-formation extraction and timestamp normalization. We adopt a two-stage processing framework in which the Whisper-Large-v3 model is used for speech-to-text conversion, with speech recognition accuracy further improved through noise reduction techniques. Subsequently, we use the Mistral-7B-Instruct pre-trained model, combined with Low-Rank Adaptation fine-tuning, to enhance sensitive information extraction. To improve annotation accuracy, ChatGPT is introduced for non-parametric semantic extraction. Experimental results demonstrate that the generative model outperforms traditional discriminative models in SHI extraction tasks. The results indicate that the proposed method performs well in both sensitive information extraction and timestamp normalization, supporting AI applications in healthcare data privacy protection and management.

Keywords: Generative Models · Sensitive Health Information Extraction · Speech-to-Text · Timestamp Normalization · LoRA Fine-Tuning · ChatGPT

1 Introduction

Generative Artificial Intelligence and Natural Language Processing (NLP) has made Large Language Models (LLMs) a key driver of industrial transformation. These technologies are expected to significantly transform the healthcare sector. LLM-based applications have already emerged in clinical settings, enhancing patient care, simplifying administrative processes, and supporting medical research. In healthcare, AI-driven systems can analyze large volumes of clinical data, including electronic health records (EHRs), medical imaging, and genetic information, to support diagnosis, treatment planning, and personalized medicine [1].

Recent benchmarking efforts have demonstrated the growing utility of LLMs in clinical de-identification and temporal normalization tasks [2]. The SREDH/AI CUP

© The Author(s), under exclusive license to Springer Nature Singapore Pte Ltd. 2026
J. Jonnagaddala et al. (Eds.): IW-DMRN 2025, CCIS 2908, pp. 59–67, 2026.
https://doi.org/10.1007/978-981-92-2282-7_5

2023 competition evaluated these capabilities using 3,244 pathology reports annotated with surrogated sensitive health informations (SHIs) and normalized dates, attracting 291 teams, with top submissions achieving macro-F1 scores exceeding 0.8. Notably, 77.2% of participating teams employed LLMs, underscoring their increasing adoption in healthcare NLP. Findings from this competition, presented at the IW-DMRN workshop in 2024, revealed that fine-tuning with low-rank adaptation improves performance, though gains plateau or degrade in models exceeding 6B parameters due to overfitting [3]. These results highlight the importance of data augmentation, hybrid approaches, and careful training strategies. Critically, effective LLM-based de-identification must balance predictive performance with the legal and ethical requirements of regulated healthcare environments, ensuring both patient privacy and model interpretability [4].

EMRs are crucial for advancing clinical research and improving patient care. However, a major challenge in integrating LLMs into healthcare is removing SHI from sources such as doctor-patient interview records and other medical texts. This step is essential to prevent potential privacy breaches. SHI encompasses individually identifiable data related to a patient's past, present, or future physical or mental health conditions, healthcare provision, or payment for care. Under regulations such as HIPAA and GDPR, protecting this information is both a legal and ethical imperative. The extraction and anonymization of SHI are therefore clinically relevant, balancing the utility of medical data for secondary analysis with the fundamental right to patient confidentiality. To address these challenges, this study proposes a comprehensive solution. The main contributions of this study are summarized as follows:

We propose a novel two-stage framework integrating Whisper for speech-to-text conversion and Mistral-7B with LoRA for entity extraction. We introduce a hybrid generative approach incorporating ChatGPT to enhance semantic extraction, demonstrating superior performance over traditional discriminative models. Our method achieves competitive performance, ranking 18-th in the AI CUP shared task and demonstrating significant improvements in temporal normalization accuracy.

2   Methodology

2.1   Dataset

The experiments in this study were conducted using the dataset provided by the 2025 SREDH/AI CUP competition [4], hosted on CodaBench [5] and organized by the SREDH Consortium in collaboration with National Kaohsiung University of Science and Technology and Asia University. The competition comprised two sub-tasks: Sub-task 1 focused on developing Automatic Speech Recognition (ASR) technology to convert doctor-patient spoken dialogue into text, while Sub-task 2 required identifying and classifying sensitive personal information mentioned in those speech recordings according to predefined SHI categories The underlying corpus is the OpenDeID dataset, the first Australian-based gold-standard corpus designed specifically for patient de-identification, comprising 2,100 pathology reports drawn from 1,833 cancer patients, with a total of 38,414 annotated Protected Health Information (PHI) entities [6]. The corpus has been manually annotated with surrogate information to ensure the absence of any identifiable patient data, making it suitable for research into privacy-preserving clinical NLP [7, 8]. Inter-annotator agreement scores of 0.9464 and 0.9503 across de-identification settings confirm the high quality of the annotations. The dataset contains mixed Chinese and English medical speech recordings, which introduced additional challenges in language detection and transcription that our framework was designed to address.

To address challenges in extracting sensitive personal information from medical speech and normalizing temporal expressions, we propose a two-stage framework. The first stage performs ASR with noise reduction and language detection. The second stage uses an LLM fine-tuned with LoRA for sensitive SHI extraction. The overall workflow advances privacy protection and data standardization in electronic medical records.

2.2 Stage 1: Automatic Speech Recognition

We used the Whisper-Large-v3 model via the HuggingFace pipeline for speech-to-text conversion. Given that medical environments often contain background noise, the audio signals were preprocessed using the *librosa* and *noisereduce* packages [9] prior to recognition. To handle the mixed-language nature of the dataset (Chinese and English), we implemented a rule-based automatic language detection mechanism. Based on file naming conventions (files indexed above 80,000 identified as Chinese), the system dynamically adjusts the language hint passed to the Whisper model. The processing pipeline includes:

1. Loading audio at a 16 kHz sampling rate.
2. Applying noise reduction; falling back to original audio if signal degradation occurs.
3. Processing with the Whisper model using a chunk length of 60 s and dynamic stride settings.

Timestamp Enhancement with WhisperX: Since the downstream task requires precise temporal alignment, the initial token-level timestamps from Whisper-Large-v3 were insufficient. We converted the model to WhisperX format using *ctranslate2* package [10], enabling forced alignment to regenerate precise start and end times for each word. The timestamps were stored in JSON format to support the subsequent entity extraction task.

2.3 Stage 2: Sensitive Information Extraction Via LLM

Model Architecture and LoRA Fine-Tuning: For SHI extraction, we selected *Mistral-7B-Instruct-v0.2* as the base model due to its balance of inference capability and resource efficiency. To reduce the high computational cost of full-parameter training, we employed LoRA. LoRA freezes the pre-trained model weights and injects trainable rank-decomposition matrices into the Transformer layers, specifically targeting the q_proj and v_proj modules (Fig. 1). This approach significantly reduces VRAM usage while maintaining the model's generalization ability on small-sample datasets. We used the HuggingFace *peft* and *datasets* libraries [9] to implement the training pipeline.

Hyperparameter Configuration: To ensure reproducibility, the specific hyperparameters used for LoRA fine-tuning are detailed in Table 1.

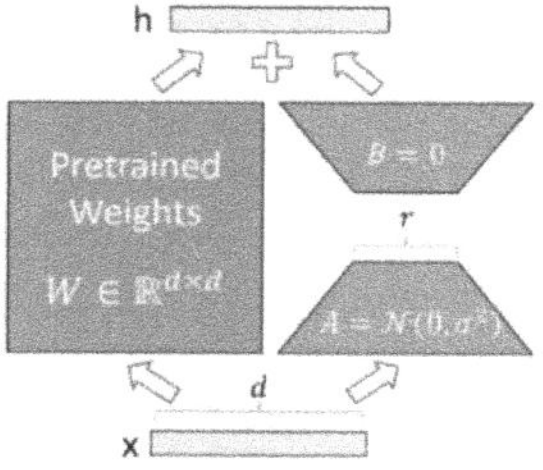

Fig. 1. Schematic diagram of the LoRA mechanism applied to the Transformer attention layers [11].

Table 1. Hyperparameters for LoRA Fine-tuning.

Parameter	Value	Description
Rank (r)	8	Dimension of the low-rank matrices
Alpha (α)	16	Scaling factor for LoRA weights
Dropout	0.05	Regularization to prevent overfitting
Learning Rate	2e-4	Step size for optimization
Batch Size	2	Per-device batch size (Accumulation steps: 8)
Epochs	10	Total training iterations
Precision	FP16	Mixed precision training

2.4 Hybrid Approach: Integrating ChatGPT for Semantic Extraction

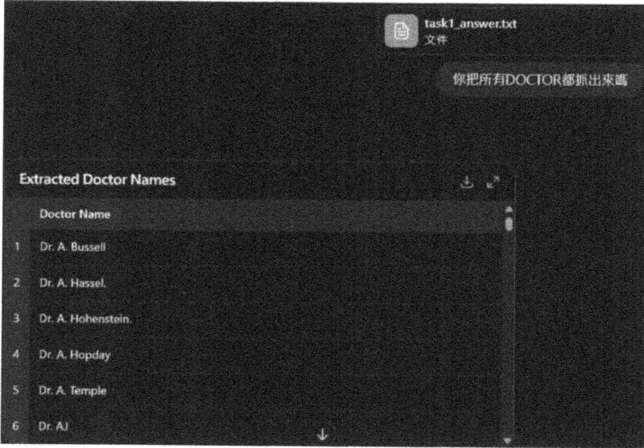

Fig. 2. Example of initial zero-shot prompt testing.

In addition to the fine-tuned Mistral model, we explored a hybrid approach by incorporating ChatGPT as a non-parametric auxiliary tool, which was particularly useful for verifying complex entities such as *DOCTOR* names. We designed a progressive prompting strategy:

Initial Prompting: Direct requests for entity lists often resulted in unstructured outputs (Fig. 2).

Structured Refinement: We refined the prompt to strictly enforce a "Filename + Label + Content" format (Fig. 3).

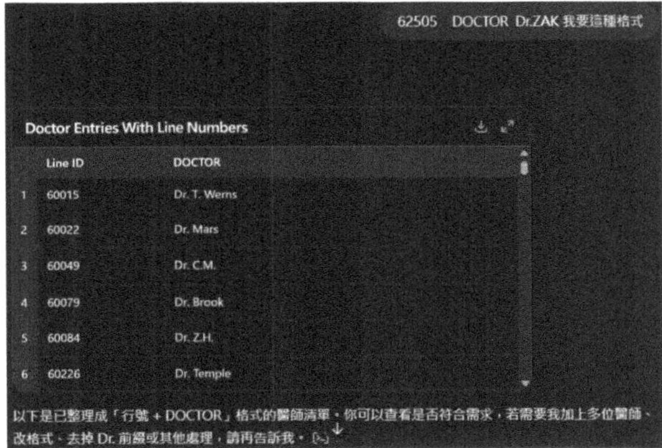

Fig. 3. Refined prompt for structured output generation.

Recall Enhancement: Further adjustments guided the model to extract all potential duplicate tags to improve recall (Fig. 4).

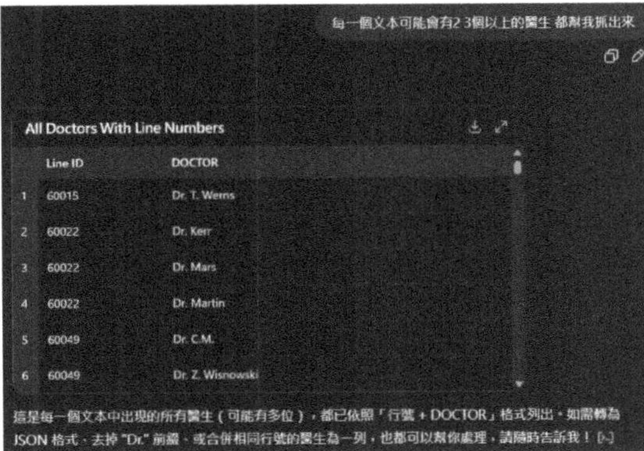

Fig. 4. Prompt optimization strategy for enhancing entity recall and capturing duplicate tags.

Structured Output and Validation Reference: To facilitate automated comparison and data integration, we instructed the model to format the final output as a structured JSON object. The output includes the file ID, entity label, and extracted text. This structured representation serves as a "silver standard" reference for validating the predictions of the fine-tuned *Mistral-7B* model (Fig. 5).

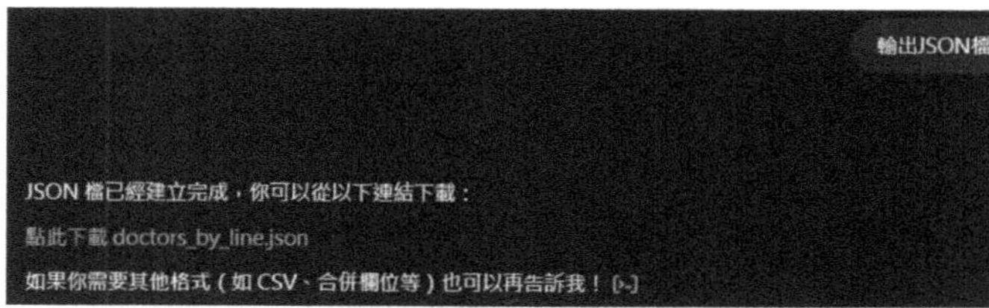

Fig. 5. Sample JSON output generated by the auxiliary ChatGPT model for cross-validation.

Through this design process, we demonstrated the auxiliary value of large language models in semi-supervised annotation. This approach not only reduces the burden of manual annotation but also validates the feasibility of future automated annotation platforms.

2.5   Data Post-processing and Output Generation

To ensure that extracted entities are mapped to precise audio timestamps, we implemented a three-step post-processing pipeline.

Entity Normalization and Merging: First, we integrated predictions from the primary LoRA-fine-tuned model with auxiliary outputs from the generative model. Rule-based pattern matching was applied to normalize specific categories such as *MEDI-CAL_RECORD_NUMBER*, *DOCTOR*, and *HOSPITAL*. This step included deduplication and consistency checks to merge overlapping entities and filter out low-confidence predictions.

Timestamp Alignment: Next, text entities were aligned with audio segments using word-level timestamps generated by WhisperX in Stage 1. A sliding-window fuzzy matching algorithm was employed to identify the corresponding start and end times. For cases where WhisperX failed to generate timestamps for sentence-final tokens, a heuristic adjustment was applied by extrapolating the end time with a 0.5-s buffer added to the last successfully aligned timestamp.

Final Output Formatting: The aligned entities were formatted to meet task requirements, including ID, entity type, start time, end time, and text. Entities that could not be aligned were logged separately for error analysis, enabling iterative refinement of the alignment algorithm.

3   Result

Quantitative Evaluation: To comprehensively assess the performance of our proposed framework, we evaluated the model using Mixed Error Rate (MER) in task1 and using Precision, Recall and F1-score as task2 evaluation criteria. In task 1, we obtained 0.18 MER. In Task 2 our final system ranked 18th, demonstrating the effectiveness of the proposed two-stage architecture. Table 2 presents the detailed results for the extracted entities.

Table 2. Performance metrics of the proposed model on the test set.

Entity Type	Precision	Recall	F1-Score
PATIENT	0.6671	0.6074	0.6358
DOCTOR	0.6372	0.7107	0.672
PHONE	0.8351	0.9951	**0.9081**
ID_NUMBER	0.6505	0.3619	0.465
AGE	0.2156	0.2963	0.2496
DATE	0.8629	0.6332	0.7304
TIME	0.4336	0.6201	0.5104
ZIP	0.7111	0.487	0.5781
...	...	...	...
Overall	0.3912	0.3922	0.3791

4   Discussion

The study shows that using a two-stage generative framework improves the accuracy of sensitive health information (SHI) extraction and temporal normalization from medical speech. Separation of automatic speech recognition (ASR) and downstream semantic processing reduces error propagation and increases the reliability of the overall system. Also, transcription quality is still one of the most important factors that will affect downstream performance; therefore, even small ASR improvements will lead to higher accuracy in entity extraction and classification [12, 13].

Leveraging a generative language model through an efficient technique to fine-tune its parameters provides for improved processing of context-based and indirectly stated clinical information than typical rule-based or machine learning approaches [14]. Ultimately, this proposed approach exhibits superior adaptability to the variability seen among different forms of clinical communications in everyday practice compared to traditional methods. Recent studies indicate that LLMs perform exceptionally well on complicated tasks associated with clinical NLP [15].

Clinical text processing, particularly temporal normalization, presents a major challenge due to the prevalence of relative and ambiguous time references. A framework has been proposed to demonstrate that it can effectively align events with standardised temporal representations for use in longitudinal analysis and clinical decision support, thereby supporting prior research into the importance of temporal reasoning in the electronic health record [16].

There are, however, limitations to consider. The performance of the model is highly dependent upon the diversity and representative characteristics of the training data, and further validation of the model's predictive accuracy in other clinical settings, language accents, and specialties is necessary. Additionally, generative models sometimes produce plausible but incorrect results, which highlights the need for validation mechanisms when using such models to develop safety-critical applications [17]. Finally, due to high computational costs and latency, both of which hinder the ability to deploy the model in real-world applications, further work should be performed to improve computational resource efficiency and speed.

Overall, the results suggest that a two-stage generative approach provides an effective and scalable method for extracting SHIs and performing temporal normalisation. The implications of this work for privacy protection through the use of data processing techniques, automated de-identification, and more efficient clinical documentation workflows are substantial. Future work should focus on enhancing the generalizability of these systems and extending them to support multiple languages; providing confidence estimation features; and enhancing user trust and desirability, all of which are critical to the success of any system used in clinical practice, as has been noted in other recent literature.

5 Conclusion

In this study, we addressed the critical challenge of extracting SHI and normalizing temporal expressions in unstructured medical records. By implementing a hybrid framework that leverages the generative capabilities of large language models with parameter-efficient LoRA fine-tuning, we successfully demonstrated that generative approaches outperform traditional methods in capturing context-dependent clinical entities. Our analysis reveals that while discriminative models often struggle with variable entity boundaries, generative models provide the flexibility needed for accurate temporal normalization. The results confirm that our approach not only ensures high extraction accuracy as evidenced by our top-tier ranking in the shared task but also offers a scalable solution for de-identifying clinical data. Future work will focus on optimizing inference speed and exploring the applicability of this framework to multilingual medical records.

The secondary use of EHRs with LLMs introduces significant privacy risks that regulatory frameworks such as GDPR and HIPAA alone cannot fully address. Complementary strategies including locally deployed privacy-preserving LLMs, synthetic data generation, differential privacy, and de-identification are essential to reduce exposure of sensitive patient information in generative AI pipelines. The appropriate combination of these strategies should be tailored to the specific task and deployment context to ensure meaningful compliance with patient privacy regulations. As demonstrated in this study, robust de-identification is a critical first step, but must be situated within a broader privacy-by-design approach to responsibly enable clinical data reuse.

Acknowledgments. This study was supported in part by the National Institute of Cancer Research, National Health Research Institutes, Tainan, Taiwan, and the Center for Big Data Research at Kaohsiung Medical University. The authors would like to thank the organizers of the AI CUP 2025 Spring competition for providing the dataset and the evaluation platform that made this research possible.

Disclosure of Interests. The authors have no competing interests to declare that are relevant to the content of this article.

References

1. Jonnagaddala, J., Wong, Z.S.-Y.: Privacy preserving strategies for electronic health records in the era of large language models. npj Digit. Med. **8**(1), 34 (2025)
2. Panchal, O., et al., Benchmarking Large Language Models for De-Identification of Electronic Health Record Notes. 2026.
3. Dai, H.-J., et al.: Leveraging large language models for the deidentification and temporal normalization of sensitive health information in electronic health records. npj Digit. Med. **8**(1), 517 (2025)
4. Dai, H.-J., et al.: Leveraging State-of-the-Art LLMs for the De-identification of Sensitive Health Information in Clinical Speech. medRxiv, p. 2026.04.13.26349911 (2026)
5. Codabench: AICUP Medical Patient Speech Sensitive Personal Data Identification Competition (2025). Available from: https://www.codabench.org/competitions/4890/.
6. Dai, H.J., et al.: A Clinical Speech Corpus with Temporally Aligned Sensitive Health Information (2026). https://www.medrxiv.org/content/10.64898/2026.03.31.26349906v2
7. Chen, A., et al.: Generation of surrogates for De-identification of electronic health records. Stud. Health Technol. Inform. **264**, 70–73 (2019)
8. Jonnagaddala, J., et al.: The OpenDeID corpus for patient de-identification. Sci. Rep. **11**(1), 19973 (2021)
9. Face, H.: openai/whisper-large-v3 (2025). Available from: https://huggingface.co/openai/whisper-large-v3.
10. Github: CTranslate2. (2025). Available from: https://github.com/OpenNMT/CTranslate2.
11. Hu, E.J., et al.: Lora: low-rank adaptation of large language models. Iclr. **1**(2), 3 (2022)
12. Radford, A., et al.: Robust Speech Recognition via Large-Scale Weak Supervision (2022)
13. Chan, W., et al.: Listen, attend and spell: a neural network for large vocabulary conversational speech recognition. In: 2016 IEEE International Conference on Acoustics, Speech and Signal Processing (ICASSP) (2016)
14. Brown, T., et al.: Language Models are Few-Shot Learners (2020)
15. Touvron, H.: et al. LLaMA, Open and Efficient Foundation Language Models (2023)
16. Uzuner, Ö., et al.: 2010 i2b2/VA challenge on concepts, assertions, and relations in clinical text. J. Am. Med. Inform. Assoc. **18**(5), 552–556 (2011)
17. Anh-Hoang, D., Tran, V., Nguyen, L.M.: Survey and analysis of hallucinations in large language models: attribution to prompting strategies or model behavior. Front. Artif. Intell. **8**, 1622292 (2025)

Recognition of Sensitive Personal Data in Doctor-Patient Speech

Bo-Han Feng[1]([✉]) [iD], Yu-Chi Cheng[1] [iD], Wen-Po Lin[1] [iD], You-Hsuan Chang[1] [iD], Vu Thinh Doan[2,3] [iD], and Kun-Pin Hsieh[4] [iD]

[1] Department of Computer Science and Information Engineering, National Taiwan University, Taipei, Taiwan
{b10902031,b10902115}@csie.ntu.edu.tw
[2] Intelligent System Laboratory, Department of Electrical Engineering, College of Electrical Engineering and Computer Science, NKUST, Kaohsiung, Taiwan
i114154107@nkust.edu.tw
[3] Faculty of Information Technology, Nha Trang University, Nha Trang, Khanh Hoa, Vietnam
[4] Department of Pharmacy, School of Pharmacy, College of Pharmacy, Kaohsiung Medical University, Kaohsiung Medical University Hospital, Kaohsiung, Taiwan
kphsieh@kmu.edu.tw

Abstract. This study addresses the automatic recognition and de-identification of Sensitive Health Information (SHI) from multilingual and spoken clinical data, a critical task for privacy-preserving healthcare analytics. We propose a comprehensive framework integrating speech recognition and Named Entity Recognition (NER), leveraging cool-whisper and parakeet-tdt-0.6b-v2 for transcription and Llama-3.2-3B-Instruct with Low-Rank Adaptation of Large Language Models (LoRA) for entity tagging. The system incorporates in-context learning, system prompts, and post-processing strategies to enhance accuracy across 23 SHI categories. Experimental results demonstrate notable improvements in macro-average F1, increasing from 0.5195 to 0.5615 (+0.042), particularly for ambiguous or variable entities, while highlighting persistent challenges for rare or sparse classes (Our code and data for this paper are made available at: https://github.com/WoZ henDeShenMeDouBuZhidao/aicup-2025.).

Keywords: Sensitive health information · Multilingual speech recognition · Named entity recognition · LoRA adapters · In-context learning

1 Introduction

Sensitive personal data in clinical settings, including patient identifiers, medical conditions, medication details, and treatment histories, is highly confidential and requires stringent protection [1]. The protection of such information is mandated by legal regulations and is fundamental to maintaining ethical standards in healthcare research and practice. In particular, doctor-patient conversations contain rich, unstructured information that plays a central role in both clinical decision-making and medical research. These conversations often include contextual descriptions, temporal expressions, and domain-specific terminology. They are an invaluable source of data for downstream tasks such as clinical outcome prediction, knowledge extraction, and decision support.

Automatic recognition and de-identification of SHI from spoken interactions have emerged as a critical research area. This urgency arises from the widespread adoption of Electronic Health Records (EHRs) following the introduction of regulatory frameworks such as the Health Insurance Portability and Accountability Act (HIPAA) in the United States and the General Data Protection Regulation (GDPR) in Europe [2]. Manual annotation is infeasible for large-scale EHRs and audio-recorded consultations due to its labor intensity, inconsistency, and limited reproducibility [3]. Consequently, automated approaches are now indispensable for supporting privacy-preserving data sharing, ensuring regulatory compliance, and enabling scalable secure natural language processing (NLP) applications in clinical domains [4].

Existing speech recognition and NER systems, however, face major challenges when applied to clinical contexts. First, multilingual audio-common in societies where code-switching between English and Chinese occurs-poses difficulties for traditional ASR systems [5]. Second, transcription noise, particularly in medical consultations with diverse accents, rapid speech, or overlapping voices, significantly reduces NER accuracy [6]. Third, clinical conversations contain highly domain-specific entities such as medication dosages, treatment timelines, or shorthand expressions, which are often absent in general-purpose corpora [7]. Conventional NER pipelines may therefore suffer from entity confusion, poor generalization across domains, and an imbalance between precision and recall. Moreover, most existing work focuses either on written English clinical text or monolingual corpora, leaving significant gaps in handling mixed-language speech and Traditional Chinese transcripts.

Building on prior editions of the AI-Cup, particularly the 2023 challenge on de-identification and temporal normalization of sensitive health information in electronic health record notes [8, 9], the current AICUP-2025 competition extends the task to multilingual spoken doctor–patient conversations. This continuity ensures comparability with previous benchmarks while introducing new challenges such as transcription noise, code-switching, and domain-specific terminology in noisy audio.

In this paper, we address the aforementioned research gaps by proposing a comprehensive approach developed for the 2025 AI-Cup Competition on SHI recognition [10]. Our method integrates multilingual speech recognition, targeted entity modeling, and robust post-processing techniques into a unified framework. Specifically, we adopt an automatic language-detection strategy, leveraging cool-whisper for Traditional Chinese and mixed-language speech, and *parakeet-tdt-0.6b-v2* [11] for English, thereby improving transcription robustness across multilingual inputs. Unicode checks are incorporated to enable task-based model routing, while rule-based duplicate-character removal mitigates systematic errors in Chinese transcripts.

For entity recognition, we employ a LoRA architecture, splitting SHI into six semantically meaningful groups for fine-tuning. This design prevents model confusion by separating easily conflated entity types and ensures balanced training between raw and tagged data to reduce bias. To further enhance robustness, we incorporate in-context learning examples and Gemini-generated entity prompts, which improve model adaptation to noisy transcriptions. Finally, we introduce alignment of transcription character indices with word-level timestamps from the speech model, enabling reliable temporal mapping of entities. Post-processing strategies, including false-positive blacklists and entity-type correction rules, are applied to further optimize performance and maximize F1 scores.

The main contributions of this paper can be highlighted as follows:

- We propose a unified framework for recognizing and de-identifying SHI from multilingual and spoken clinical data, combining speech recognition and NER in a single pipeline.
- We LoRA with a foundation model (*Llama-3.2-3B-Instruct*) to efficiently fine-tune on multiple entity categories while maintaining general linguistic knowledge.
- In-context learning and system prompts are incorporated to enhance recognition of ambiguous or variable entities, improving robustness under noisy transcription conditions.
- Post-processing strategies, including entity-specific blacklists and temporal alignment with speech timestamps, are applied to optimize performance across all SHI categories.

The remainder of this paper is organized as follows. Section 2 reviews studies on clinical de-identification and NER, with a focus on multilingual and speech-based approaches. Section 3 introduces the proposed framework for speech recognition and NER, including the use of LoRA, in-context learning, and system prompts. Section 4 describes the preprocessing, adapter-based tagging, and post-processing steps applied to the training and test data. Section 5 presents experimental results on benchmark datasets, evaluating both transcription quality and entity recognition performance. Section 6 provides a detailed analysis of the observed outcomes, highlights limitations, and explores potential strategies for further improvement. Finally, Sect. 7 summarizes the main contributions and outlines directions for future work.

2 Methods

This section reviews two main research directions related to our work: (i) generic clinical de-identification and NER methods in clinical natural language processing (Sect. 2.1), and (ii) recent advances in multilingual and speech-based de-identification approaches (Sect. 2.2).

2.1 Generic Clinical De-identification and NER Methods

Clinical de-identification has been studied for over two decades to protect patient privacy while preserving EHR utility [12]. Initial methods for clinical de-identification relied on handcrafted rules, dictionaries, and regular expressions to detect SHI [13]. These methods were straightforward to implement and interpretable but suffered from low adaptability across institutions due to vocabulary variation and ambiguous entity boundaries.

The shift toward statistical sequence labeling models such as Conditional Random Fields (CRFs) [14] and Hidden Markov Models (HMMs) provided more flexibility by incorporating contextual and linguistic features. However, these methods still required substantial feature engineering and domain knowledge, which limited scalability.

Deep learning models such as Convolutional Neural Networks (CNNs) and Bi-directional Long Short-Term Memory networks (BiLSTMs) became dominant in clinical NER and de-identification task [15, 16]. These architectures alleviated the need for manual feature design by learning hierarchical and contextual representations directly from data, but their performance remained limited by data scarcity, a common challenge in healthcare.

However, benchmarking large language models (LLMs) is essential for systematically evaluating their performance across standardized datasets and tasks. Such benchmarks enable objective comparison of different models and help assess their robustness, generalization ability, and suitability for domain-specific applications such as clinical information extraction and de-identification [17].

Recent work has also explored surrogate generation techniques for privacy-preserving clinical text processing. Chen et al. [18]. propose a framework for generating realistic surrogate data to replace sensitive identifiers in electronic health records (EHRs), enabling de-identified datasets to retain linguistic and contextual coherence while protecting patient privacy. Their approach systematically substitutes sensitive attributes such as names, locations, and identifiers with contextually plausible alternatives, thereby preserving the structural and semantic properties of the original records. This strategy improves the utility of de-identified datasets for downstream natural language processing tasks, including named entity recognition and clinical information extraction, while ensuring compliance with privacy protection requirements.

Other studies have applied transformer-based architectures to clinical de-identification. BERT, BioBERT, and ClinicalBERT have significantly improved the accuracy and robustness of de-identification systems [19, 20]. These models leverage large-scale biomedical corpora and contextual embeddings to capture subtle semantic cues, thereby outperforming traditional deep learning methods. Despite these successes, most existing work still focuses on English clinical text, leaving multilingual and spoken data underexplored.

2.2 De-identification for Multilingual and Spoken Clinical Data

Rule-based approaches have been widely employed in early attempts to de-identify SHI from spoken clinical interactions and multilingual data. In [21, 22], authors developed systems that relied on handcrafted dictionaries, regular expressions, and pattern-matching rules to detect SHI, such as patient names, dates, locations, and identifiers. These approaches achieved high precision and interpretability but were limited by their dependence on language-specific resources and by low adaptability in multilingual or code-switched speech contexts. Moreover, transcription noise, common in audio recordings of doctor–patient conversations, often caused significant degradation in performance.

Statistical sequence labeling models, including CRFs and HMMs, were later introduced to improve generalization and handle contextual dependencies [14]. By incorporating linguistic and temporal features, these models could identify entities beyond rigid pattern matches. For instance, CRFs were successfully applied to English clinical texts to extract PHI with improved recall compared to rule-based methods. However, their reliance on extensive feature engineering and domain expertise still limited scalability, particularly for multilingual corpora or low-resource languages.

Deep learning architectures, notably BiLSTMs and CNNs, have demonstrated superior performance in both text and speech-based de-identification [15, 16]. These models automatically learn hierarchical and contextual representations from data, reducing the need for manual feature design. More recently, transformer-based models, such as BERT, BioBERT, and ClinicalBERT, have achieved state-of-the-art results for clinical entity recognition [19, 20], including multilingual settings. Researchers have also proposed speech-aware NER systems combining automatic speech recognition (ASR) with contextual embeddings [5–7]. These systems address code-switching scenarios between English and Chinese, and improve recognition of domain-specific entities in noisy audio. Benchmarks on multilingual spoken clinical datasets have revealed that integrating ASR with transformer-based NER substantially improves entity detection and temporal alignment, which is critical for downstream applications such as anonymization and selective redaction.

Recent multilingual and speech-centric frameworks extend these methods by leveraging pretraining on both textual and spoken biomedical corpora. For example, Xue et al. [23] introduced a multilingual BERT-based model fine-tuned on English-Chinese clinical dialogues, achieving higher F1 scores on SHI extraction tasks. Similarly, Mdhaffar et al. [24] proposed an end-to-end speech-to-entity model that jointly optimizes ASR and NER objectives, demonstrating robustness to transcription errors and accent variation. Such approaches illustrate the current trend toward unified, automated de-identification systems capable of handling large-scale, multilingual clinical audio, bridging the gap between traditional text-based NER and real-world spoken data.

Recent benchmark efforts have further advanced multilingual and speech-based de-identification. Notably, the AI-Cup 2023 focused on de-identification and temporal normalization of sensitive health information in electronic health record notes. Mir et al. reported that large language models achieved macro-F1 scores of 0.912 for SHI recognition and 0.869 for temporal normalization, substantially outperforming traditional baselines [9]. Dai et al. highlighted that 77% of participating teams leveraged LLMs, often in combination with rule-based strategies, underscoring the growing role of foundation models in clinical NLP [8]. These works established the annotation schema of eight major groups and 31 subcategories of SHI, as well as standardized temporal formats (ISO 8601), which serve as the basis for subsequent AI-Cup challenges. In contrast to the 2023 edition, which focused on textual EHR notes, the 2025 AI-Cup [25] expands the scope to multilingual spoken doctor–patient conversations, introducing new challenges such as transcription noise, code-switching between English and Traditional Chinese, and recognition of domain-specific entities in noisy audio.

Complementary to these benchmark efforts, Kim et al. [26] introduced a multi-layered framework that integrates ClinicalBERT with rule-based strategies for free-text medical records, demonstrating improved performance across multiple languages. Wiest et al. [27] leveraged privacy-preserving large language models to de-identify multilingual medical documents, highlighting the feasibility of secure LLM deployment in healthcare.

2.3 Proposed Clinical Data Processing Tasks

This section introduces the proposed detection framework, which integrates the speech recognition pipeline (Sect. 3.1) and the NER framework (Sect. 3.2).

Speech Recognition Task

We propose a prediction pipeline that employs the cool-whisper model to generate initial transcriptions for all audio files, handling both English and mixed English–Traditional Chinese speech (Fig. 1). A Unicode-based detection module then examines each transcription to identify the presence of Chinese characters. Transcriptions containing Chinese characters are classified as Traditional Chinese speech and retain the cool-whisper output, whereas audio segments without Chinese characters are re-processed using *parakeet-tdt-0.6b-v2*, which is specialized for English speech recognition.

Structured entities such as MEDICALRECORD or IDNUM frequently appear in English audio, which un-fine-tuned speech recognition models fail to transcribe correctly. To address this, *parakeet-tdt-0.6b-v2* is fine-tuned on the competition training set, improving transcription accuracy for segments originally transcribed entirely in English by cool-whisper. Instances where characters are not covered by the model vocabulary can result in blank or unstable outputs; in such cases, the original cool-whisper transcription is retained.

Both cool-whisper and *parakeet-tdt-0.6b-v2* are relatively lightweight models with 600 M and approximately 750 M parameters, respectively. In addition to transcriptions, both models provide word-level timestamps indicating entity start and end times, which are classified and filtered according to the same rules applied to the transcription outputs.

For fine-tuning *parakeet-tdt-0.6b-v2*, we employed NVIDIA *NeMo's speech_to_text_finetune* pipeline. The model was initialized from the official ".nemo" checkpoint and trained on the competition training set, which consisted of approximately 10 h of English audio. Data were split speaker-independently into 80% training, 10% validation, and 10% test sets. We retained the tokenizer from the pretrained checkpoint (update_tokenizer = False) to ensure consistency with the original vocabulary.

Training was performed for up to 50 epochs with AdamW optimizer (learning rate 1e-4, betas = (0.9, 0.98), weight decay = 1e-3) and a CosineAnnealing scheduler (warmup = 5000 steps, minimum learning rate 5e-6). Batch size was set to 32 with gradient accumulation of 2, precision 32, and training conducted on a GPU. SpecAugment was applied with 2 frequency masks (width = 27) and 10 time masks (width = 0.05) to improve robustness. Validation was performed once per epoch, and the best checkpoints were selected based on minimum word error rate (WER).

Named Entity Recognition Task

We propose a NER framework that processes all entity types grouped into six major categories (Fig. 2). A single foundation model is employed alongside six LoRA adapters, each specialized for one entity category. For each raw transcription, the foundation

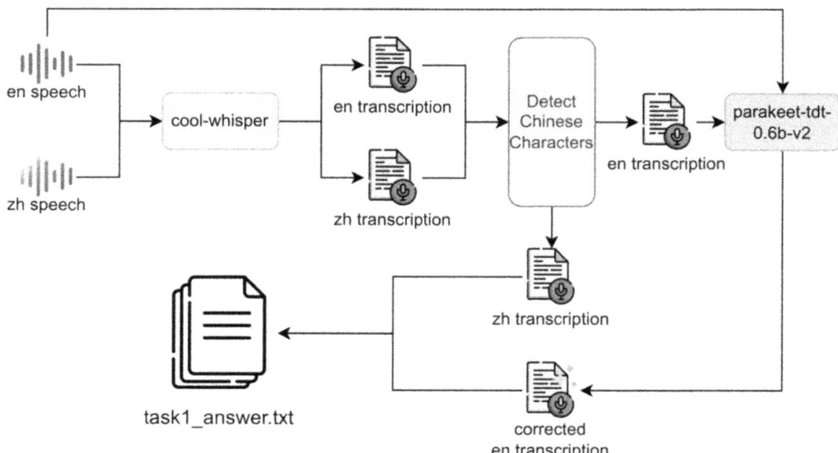

Fig. 1. Prediction pipeline for the speech recognition task.

model and adapters operate in parallel, with each adapter identifying entities within its designated category and wrapping them with corresponding special tokens, producing a tagged transcription.

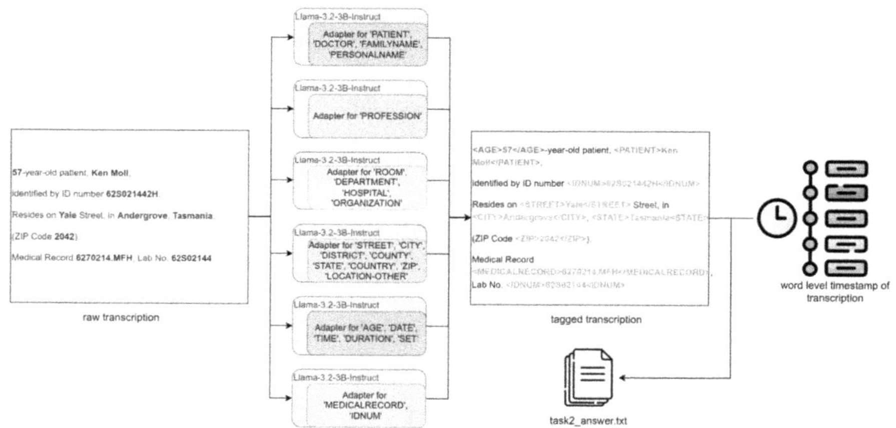

Fig. 2. Prediction pipeline for the NER task.

Tagged transcriptions from all adapter-model combinations are aggregated to obtain recognition results across all entity categories for a single raw transcription. Entity boundaries are determined by locating the surrounding special tokens. Each recognized entity is then mapped to the corresponding audio timesteps obtained from the speech recognition task, with each segment represented as a 3-tuple [text content, start time, end time]. By identifying the segments corresponding to the start and end indices of the entity, accurate temporal alignment is achieved, resulting in a fully annotated transcription.

The foundation model utilized for this task is *Llama-3.2-3B-Instruct* [24]. The model's core parameters are kept frozen during training, and six LoRA adapters corresponding to the entity categories are fine-tuned. This design enables efficient adaptation to multiple entity types while leveraging the general linguistic knowledge encoded in the foundation model.

We applied parameter-efficient fine-tuning via LoRA on the *Llama-3.2-3B-Instruct* backbone. Adapters were inserted into the *up_proj, down_proj, gate_proj, q_proj, k_proj, v_proj*, and *o_proj* modules. We used rank r = 16, scaling α = 32, and dropout = 0.1, with bias disabled. For quantization, we employed QLoRA with 4-bit NF4 quantization, double quantization enabled, and bfloat16 as the compute dtype using the bitsandbytes backend. This configuration reduced memory usage while preserving model performance.

2.4 Data Processing

Dataset

We used SREDH-AICup SHI speech corpus 2025.The corpus is divided into three subsets: a training set of 1,539 files totaling approximately 10 h, a validation set of 775 files with about 5 h, and a test set of 710 files also covering 5 h. In total, the dataset comprises 3,024 files with a cumulative duration of roughly 20 h, ensuring a balanced distribution for model training, hyperparameter tuning, and final evaluation [28] (Table 1).

Table 1. Summary of dataset subsets

Subset	Duration (hours)	File
Training	10	1539
Validation	5	775
Test	5	710

Table 2 presents the distribution of annotated entity categories across the training, validation, and test subsets of the corpus. The dataset covers a wide range of sensitive and contextual information, including patient identifiers (e.g., PATIENT, DOCTOR, PERSONALNAME, FAMILYNAME), institutional references (HOSPITAL, DEPARTMENT, ORGANIZATION), and location-related attributes (CITY, STATE, ZIP, COUNTRY, STREET). Temporal expressions (DATE, TIME, DURATION, SET) and numerical identifiers (MEDICAL_RECORD_NUMBER, ID_NUMBER, PHONE, URL) are also represented.

Overall, the corpus contains 3,024 annotated instances distributed across 25 entity types, with the largest categories being DATE (1,811 instances), DOCTOR (1,365 instances), and PATIENT (828 instances). This balanced yet diverse distribution ensures that the dataset supports comprehensive evaluation of entity recognition models, particularly in the medical and administrative domains [29].

Table 2. SHI category statistics

	Training Set	Validation Set	Test set	Total
PATIENT	178	182	468	828
DOCTOR	227	306	832	1365
PERSONALNAME	194	46	4	244
FAMILYNAME	146	28	12	186
PROFESSION	26	16	2	44
HOSPITAL	40	73	167	280
DEPARTMENT	39	67	135	241
ROOM	3	0	2	5
STREET	24	64	116	204
CITY	55	65	120	240
DISTRICT	0	1	0	1
COUNTY	2	2	0	4
STATE	40	64	111	215
ZIP	22	60	115	197
COUNTRY	11	3	2	16
ORGANIZATION	20	12	6	38
LOCATION-OTHER	11	6	4	21
AGE	40	17	34	91
DATE	668	493	650	1811
TIME	171	110	125	406
DURATION	336	152	8	496
SET	41	29	8	78
MEDICAL_RECORD_NUMBER	31	68	158	257
ID_NUMBER	60	175	324	559
PHONE	1	0	1	2
URL	1	0	0	1

Preprocessing Strategies

The training data for the speech recognition task (Task 1) did not undergo any special preprocessing. The only processing applied was filtering English audio files (Fig. 1), for fine-tuning *parakeet-tdt-0.6b-v2*.

After generating the Task 1 prediction files, some transcriptions produced by cool-whisper for mixed Traditional Chinese audio contained a single character repeated more than five times consecutively. These excessive repetitions were removed using a rule-based post-processing step to obtain the final Task 1 prediction files.

In the NER task, all entity types were grouped into multiple categories, each assigned to a dedicated LoRA adapter. During prediction, each adapter only outputs a tagged transcription corresponding to its assigned entity categories.

For example, suppose the raw transcription of a single audio sample is as follows:

Example of raw transcription

57-year-old patient, Ken Moll,
identified by ID number 62S021442H.
Resides on Yale Street, in Andergrove, Tasmania.
(ZIP Code 2042).
Medical Record 6270214.MFH, Lab No. 62S02144.

Each adapter receives the raw transcription as input and outputs a tagged transcription, enclosing only the entities it handles in special tokens. Figure 3 illustrates these adapter outputs. Output sequences generated by the adapters may match the raw transcription when no entities of the corresponding category are detected. To maintain a balanced distribution between tagged and untagged transcriptions, a subset of these identical outputs is randomly discarded, ensuring that tagged outputs remain predominant. We fine-tuned the models using the pre-processed and formatted training data. After obtaining outputs, we applied two post-processing steps to generate the final Task 2 submission files:

Step 1 involves constructing a category-specific blacklist. The initial predictions from Task 2 are analyzed to identify frequently occurring false positives. These entries are then incorporated into the blacklist and excluded in subsequent prediction iterations, thereby improving the overall accuracy.

- The PROFESSION category filters out strings such as Dr., patient, doctor, and physician.
- The DURATION category filters out strings like mm and semester.
- The ZIP category filters out strings that do not match a four-digit numeric format.

Step 2 corrects misclassified entities within an adapter. For instance, in the outputs of the Adapter for 'AGE', 'DATE', 'TIME', 'DURATION', and 'SET', the phrase "every day" may be labeled as 'DATE' or 'TIME'; it should be corrected to 'SET'.

2.5 Experiments and Analysis

Implementation Details

For the speech-to-text fine-tuning experiments, audio was standardized to a sample rate of 16 kHz. Training and validation were conducted with a batch size of 2, using manifests specifying the respective subsets. Utterances shorter than 0.1 s or longer than 35 s were excluded. Data augmentation was applied via SpecAugment with 2 frequency masks (width 27) and 10-time masks (width 0.05). A SentencePiece tokenizer (BPE) was employed for subword modeling. Optimization was performed using AdamW with a learning rate of 1×10^{-4}, betas (0.9,0.98), and weight decay of 1×10^{-3}. A cosine

---

PATIENT, DOCTOR, FAMILYNAME, PERSONALNAME

57-year-old patient, <PATIENT>Ken Moll</PATIENT>, identified by ID number 62S021442H. Resides on Yale Street, in Andergrove, Tasmania. (ZIP Code 2042). Medical Record 6270214.MFH, Lab No. 62S02144.

PROFESSION

57-year-old patient, Ken Moll, identified by ID number 62S021442H. Resides on Yale Street, in Andergrove, Tasmania. (ZIP Code 2042). Medical Record 6270214.MFH, Lab No. 62S02144.

ROOM, DEPARTMENT, HOSPITAL, ORGANIZATION

57-year-old patient, Ken Moll, identified by ID number 62S021442H. Resides on Yale Street, in Andergrove, Tasmania. (ZIP Code 2042). Medical Record 6270214.MFH, Lab No. 62S02144.

STREET, CITY, STATE, ZIP

57-year-old patient, Ken Moll, identified by ID number 62S021442H. Resides on <STREET>Yale</STREET> Street, in <CITY>Andergrove</CITY>, <STATE>Tasmania</STATE>. (ZIP Code <ZIP>2042</ZIP>). Medical Record 6270214.MFH, Lab No. 62S02144.

AGE, DATE, TIME, DURATION

<AGE>57</AGE>-year-old patient, Ken Moll, identified by ID number 62S021442H. Resides on Yale Street, in Andergrove, Tasmania. (ZIP Code 2042). Medical Record 6270214.MFH, Lab No. 62S02144.

MEDICALRECORD, IDNUM

57-year-old patient, Ken Moll, identified by ID number <IDNUM>62S021442H</IDNUM>. Medical Record <MEDICALRECORD>6270214.MFH</MEDICALRECORD>, Lab No. <IDNUM>62S02144</IDNUM>.

Fig. 3. Examples of adapter outputs.

annealing scheduler with 5,000 warmup steps and a minimum learning rate of 5×10^{-6} was used to stabilize training.

2.6 Speech Recognition Task

Speech Recognition Task: For Task 1, we fine-tuned *parakeet-tdt-0.6b-v2* on the English audio dataset using NVIDIA NeMo. At each epoch, a checkpoint was saved, and the validation Word Error Rate (WER) was computed. The checkpoint with the lowest WER was selected to generate predictions on the test set. During inference, each audio segment was encoded into features and decoded into tokens with durations to form sentences. Training employed a Transducer loss to align predictions with the ground truth.

NER Task: For Task 2, we fine-tuned a 4-bit quantized *Llama-3.2-3B-Instruct* using QLoRA, updating only the adapter parameters while freezing the base model. Checkpoints were saved at every epoch, and the one with the lowest validation loss was selected for final predictions. During inference, the model tokenized the input transcription and processed it through multiple Transformer layers. Self-attention and contextual embeddings were applied to generate output autoregressively until an end-of-sequence token or maximum length was reached, resulting in the final annotated transcription.

3 Results

Task 1 (Speech Recognition): the baseline models produced frequent errors when encountering characters outside of their vocabularies or domain-specific medical terminology.

Table 3 illustrates the impact of incorporating in-context learning on the recognition of SHI entity types. Across all evaluated categories, the macro-average F-Measure increased from 0.5195 without in-context learning to 0.5615 with in-context learning, reflecting a consistent improvement in the model's ability to correctly identify entities under noisy transcription conditions. This overall gain of 0.042 indicates that providing explicit input–output examples helps the model align its predictions more effectively with complex or ambiguous text patterns.

When examining individual entity categories, notable improvements were observed for PERSONALNAME, which achieved an F-Measure of 0.4222 without in-context learning and increased to 0.5206 with in-context learning. AGE also benefited substantially, rising from 0.4749 to 0.6562, indicating that entities with frequently ambiguous or variable forms gain from additional contextual examples. Geographic identifiers exhibited measurable enhancement as well: CITY increased from 0.4779 to 0.5831, COUNTRY from 0.3688 to 0.6109, and ZIP improved from 0.6582 to 0.8439. Among these, ZIP achieved one of the largest relative gains, suggesting that entities with structured but highly variable formats particularly benefit from contextual guidance.

In contrast, entities that are well-defined or consistently formatted showed only minor changes. Specifically, DATE decreased slightly from 0.9011 without in-context learning to 0.8963 with in-context learning, while MEDICALRECORD exhibited a modest increase from 0.9181 to 0.9380. These observations indicate that the benefits of in-context learning are most pronounced for entities with high variability or ambiguous forms, whereas categories that the model already recognizes reliably experience limited gains.

Table 3. F-Measure of SHI Types with and without In-Context Learning.

SHI Type	w/o In-Context	w/ In-Context
PATIENT	0.7194	0.7222
DOCTOR	0.7510	0.7553
PERSONALNAME	0.4222	0.5206
FAMILYNAME	0.5621	0.3395
PROFESSION	0.0914	0.1582
DEPARTMENT	0.6452	0.6357
HOSPITAL	0.6217	0.6436
ORGANIZATION	0.3928	0.3702
STREET	0.6686	0.6601
CITY	0.4779	0.5831
STATE	0.6318	0.7560
COUNTRY	0.3688	0.6109
COUNTY	0.0000	0.0000
ZIP	0.6582	0.8439
LOCATION-OTHER	0.0000	0.0000
AGE	0.4749	0.6562
DATE	0.9011	0.8963
TIME	0.7773	0.7597
DURATION	0.5341	0.5478
SET	0.4747	0.6488
MEDICALRECORD	0.9181	0.9380
IDNUM	0.8578	0.8691
Macro-average	**0.5195**	**0.5615**

Not all categories benefited uniformly. FAMILYNAME decreased from 0.5621 to 0.3395, and minor declines were observed for DEPARTMENT (0.6452 to 0.6357) and TIME (0.7773 to 0.7597). These reductions may be explained by insufficient training examples, confounding overlaps with semantically similar entities, or sensitivity to entity grouping strategies. Additionally, certain rare categories such as COUNTY and LOCATION-OTHER remained at 0.0000 in both conditions, highlighting persistent challenges in recognizing extremely sparse classes.

Task 2 (NER): different optimization strategies led to measurable improvements in F-Measure.

The results presented in Table 4 illustrate the impact of incorporating a system prompt on the recognition of SHI entity types. Overall, the macro-average F-Measure increased from 0.4464 without the system prompt to 0.4691 with the system prompt, indicating a consistent improvement across multiple categories. This gain of approximately 2.3 points suggests that providing explicit guidance regarding entity format and examples helps the model generate more accurate tagged transcriptions.

Table 4. Comparison of F-Measure with and without System Prompt.

SHI Type	w/o System Prompt	w/ System Prompt
PATIENT	0.7012	0.7673
DOCTOR	0.7320	0.7334
PERSONALNAME	0.0000	0.0000
FAMILYNAME	0.0309	0.0761
PROFESSION	0.0000	0.0000
ROOM	0.0000	0.0000
DEPARTMENT	0.4645	0.5096
HOSPITAL	0.5807	0.6003
ORGANIZATION	0.2282	0.3702
STREET	0.6722	0.5954
CITY	0.5596	0.5565
STATE	0.6920	0.6607
COUNTRY	0.0000	0.0000
ZIP	0.7760	0.7703
LOCATION-OTHER	0.0000	0.0000
AGE	0.6169	0.7954
DATE	0.9296	0.9246
TIME	0.8464	0.8309
DURATION	0.3970	0.3367
SET	0.3712	0.5795
PHONE	0.0000	0.0000
MEDICALRECORD	0.8819	0.8956
IDNUM	0.7877	0.7870
Macro-average	**0.4464**	**0.4691**

Entity types demonstrated measurable improvements after incorporating the system prompt. Specifically, PATIENT increased from 0.7012 to 0.7673, and FAMILY-NAME rose from 0.0309 to 0.0761, indicating that additional contextual instructions helped clarify entity boundaries. ORGANIZATION improved from 0.2282 to 0.3702, AGE increased from 0.6169 to 0.7954, and SET rose from 0.3712 to 0.5795, reflecting enhanced recognition for entities prone to ambiguity or variable textual formats. Well-defined entities such as MEDICALRECORD also showed slight gains, with the F-Measure increasing from 0.8819 to 0.8956 (Table 4).

In contrast, several entity types exhibited negligible change or no improvement following the introduction of the system prompt. Categories such as PERSONALNAME, PROFESSION, ROOM, COUNTRY, LOCATION-OTHER, and PHONE remained at zero, highlighting the persistent difficulty of identifying extremely sparse or underrepresented classes. Additionally, a few entities experienced slight reductions in performance; for example, STREET decreased from 0.6722 to 0.5954, and TIME from 0.8464 to 0.8309. These observations suggest that while the system prompt enhances recognition for ambiguous or variable entities, it may introduce minor inconsistencies for categories that are already well-established within the model's predictions.

4   Discussion

The results highlight several challenges and opportunities for improvement in both the speech recognition and NER tasks. For speech recognition, the main source of error stemmed from vocabulary mismatches. The model *parakeet-tdt-0.6b-v2* frequently produced blank tokens or *??* symbols when encountering characters outside its vocabulary. Normalizing the English training data to account for these cases could help reduce such errors. In addition, the *Cool-whisper* model, which was trained on limited Traditional Chinese data, was applied directly to the Traditional Chinese test set without fine-tuning. This resulted in suboptimal transcription quality, particularly for medical terminology such as "anesthesia" and "computed tomography". Replacing unreliable outputs with blanks, rather than retaining low-quality text, may represent a practical strategy for reducing overall error rates.

For the NER task, the choice of model proved decisive. Models such as *MedGemma* [30] and *Qwen3* [31], although strong in their respective domains, produced irrelevant tokens or tool-use artifacts that disrupted entity alignment. In contrast, *Llama-3.2-3B-Instruct*, trained solely on text, provided a more stable foundation for fine-tuning with LoRA adapters. Beyond model selection, data balancing between raw and tagged transcriptions strongly influenced performance. Training exclusively on raw or tagged transcriptions produced skewed results, with low recall or precision, respectively, whereas a balanced 50:50 ratio improved both consistency and accuracy.

Entity grouping also played an important role. When entity categories prone to confusion were trained together, such as AGE, DATE, TIME, DURATION, and SET, the model achieved higher accuracy by learning their distinctions more effectively. Conversely, grouping entities based only on surface-level similarities, such as ZIP with IDNUM and MEDICALRECORD, increased misclassifications and degraded overall performance. The use of in-context learning further enhanced model robustness. By adding examples that included noisy transcription patterns (e.g.,??, ellipses) to the training data, the model learned to align its outputs with the imperfect structure of raw transcriptions. This strategy improved macro-average F-Measure by approximately four points, showing its potential as a simple but effective technique.

The introduction of system prompts yielded smaller gains overall but demonstrated notable improvements in certain categories, particularly ORGANIZATION and AGE. This finding suggests that providing contextual explanations and examples for entity types may help mitigate ambiguity, even if the global effect remains limited. Finally, the use of data augmentation offers promising future directions. *GPT-4o-mini* or *Gemini-2.5-flash* can generate synthetic text with reliable entity annotations, which can be converted into audio using open-source TTS tools like *CosyVoice* or *BreezyVoice*. Such augmentation could extend coverage of rare entity types and increase the robustness of both recognition tasks at relatively low cost.

5 Conclusion

In this study, we proposed a framework for recognizing and de-identifying SHI from multilingual and spoken clinical data. By combining speech recognition, foundation models with LoRA adapters, in-context learning, and system prompts, the system achieves notable improvements in F-Measure, especially for entities with ambiguous or variable formats such as PATIENT, AGE, ORGANIZATION, and SET.

In-context learning enhances robustness under noisy transcriptions, and system prompts aid the classification of challenging categories. Rare entities like PERSONAL-NAME, PROFESSION, and PHONE remain difficult to detect, indicating areas for future improvement. Key factors for effective SHI recognition include careful entity grouping, balanced training between raw and tagged transcriptions, and temporal alignment from speech recognition.

Overall, the framework offers a scalable solution for multilingual, speech-based clinical NER. Future work will focus on extending coverage of rare entities, improving transcription quality for low-resource languages, and exploring joint optimization of speech and entity recognition components.

Although our experiments show improvements in F-measure, we did not include direct baseline comparisons due to differences in task scope and modality. Prior baselines focus on textual EHR notes, while our setup targets multilingual spoken conversations. Future work will establish unified benchmarks to enable direct quantitative comparison.

Acknowledgments. This work was supported by the Ministry of Education and the National Science and Technology Council under grant *NSTC112-2221-E-992-056-MY3*.

Disclosure of Interests. The authors declare that they have no competing interests relevant to the content of this article.

References

1. Heart, T., Ben-Assuli, O., Shabtai, I.: A review of PHR, EMR and EHR integration: a more personalized healthcare and public health policy. Health Policy Technol. (2017)

2. Zirikly, A., Desmet, B., Newman-Griffis, D.: Information Extraction Framework for Disability Determination Using a Mental Functioning Use-Case. JMIR Med. Inform. (2022)
3. Neamatullah, I., Douglass, M.M., Lehman, L.W.H.: Automated de-identification of free-text medical records. BMC Med. Inform. Decis. Mak. (2008)
4. Jonnagaddala, J., Wong, Z.S.-Y.: Privacy preserving strategies for electronic health records in the era of large language models. npj Digit. Med. **8**(1), 34 (2025)
5. Szymanski, P., Augustyniak, L., Morzy, M.: Why Aren't We NER Yet? Artifacts of ASR Errors in Named Entity Recognition in Spontaneous Speech Transcripts. ACL (2023)
6. King, A.J., Angus, D.C., Cooper, G.F.: A voice-based digital assistant for intelligent prompting of evidence-based practices during ICU rounds. J. Biomed. Inform. (2023)
7. Hu, Z., Li, W., Yang, H.: Named entity recognition in online medical consultation using deep learning. Appl. Sci. (2025)
8. Dai, H.-J., et al.: Leveraging large language models for the deidentification and temporal normalization of sensitive health information in electronic health records. npj Digit. Med. **8**(1), 517 (2025)
9. Mir, T.H., Yang, H.P., Chou, Y.Y.: Deidentification and Temporal Normalization of the Electronic Health Record Notes Using Large Language Models. CCIS (2025)
10. Cup, A.I.: Doctor-Patient Speech Sensitive Personal Data Recognition. AI-Cup Competition (2025)
11. Nvidia: parakeet-tdt-0.6b-v2. HuggingFace (2025)
12. Garfinkel, S.L.: De-Identification of Personal Information. NIST (2015)
13. Uzuner, O., Luo, Y., Szolovits, P.: Evaluating the state-of-the-art in automatic De-identification. J. Am. Med. Inform. Assoc. (2007)
14. Lafferty, J., McCallum, A., Pereira, F.: Conditional Random Fields: Probabilistic Models for Segmenting and Labeling Sequence. ICML (2001)
15. Lample, G., Ballesteros, M., Subramanian, S.: Neural architectures for named entity recognition. arXiv (2016)
16. Dernoncourt, F., Lee, J.Y., Uzuner, O.: De-identification of patient notes with recurrent neural networks. JAMIA (2017)
17. Panchal, O., et al.: Benchmarking Large Language Models for De-identification of Electronic Health Record Notes (2026)
18. Chen, A., et al.: Generation of surrogates for De-identification of electronic health records. Stud. Health Technol. Inform. **264**, 70–73 (2019)
19. Lee, J., Yoon, W., Kim, S.: BioBERT: a pre-trained biomedical language representation model for biomedical text mining. Bioinformatics (2020)
20. Alsentzer, E., Murphy, J., Boag, W.: Publicly available clinical BERT embeddings. Clinical NLP Workshop (2019)
21. Sweeney, L.: Replacing personally-identifying information in medical records, the scrub system. In: AMIA Symposium (1996)
22. Gupta, D., Saul, M., Gilbertson, J.: Evaluation of a deidentification software engine to share pathology reports and clinical documents for research. Am. J. Clin. Pathol. (2004)
23. Xue, K., Y. Zhou, Z. Ma: Fine-tuning BERT for joint entity and relation extraction in Chinese medical text. arXiv (2019)
24. Mdhaffar, S., Duret, J., Parcollet, T.: End-to-End Model for Named Entity Recognition from Speech without Paired Training Data. ISCA (2022)
25. Dai, H.-J., et al.: Leveraging State-of-the-art llms for the de-identification of sensitive health information in clinical speech. medRxiv. p. 2026.04.13.26349911 (2026)
26. Kim, W., Hahm, S., Lee, J.: Generalizing Clinical De-Identification Models by Privacy-Safe Data Augmentation Using GPT-4. EMNLP (2024)
27. Wiest, I.C., Westphalen, C.B., Wermke, M.: Deidentifying Medical Documents with Local Privacy-Preserving Large Language Models: the LLM-Anonymizer. NEJM AI (2024)

28. Jonnagaddala, J., et al.: The OpenDeID corpus for patient de-identification. Sci. Rep. **11**(1), 19973 (2021)
29. Dai, H.J., et al.: A Clinical Speech Corpus with Temporally Aligned Sensitive Health Information (2026). https://www.medrxiv.org/content/10.64898/2026.03.31.26349906v2
30. Google: MedGemma 4B. HuggingFace (2025)
31. Alibaba: Qwen3-8B. HuggingFace (2025)

Multistage Automatic Speech Recognition-Named Entity Recognition Framework for Privacy Sensitive Information Recognition in Medical Speech Data

Yan-Jun Chen[1] , Ting-Yi Chang[1,2] , and Tao-Hsing Chang[1(✉)]

[1] National Kaohsiung University of Science and Technology, Kaohsiung 807, Taiwan
`{c110151154,changth}@nkust.edu.tw`
[2] National Cheng Kung University, Tainan 701, Taiwan

Abstract. The semantic analysis of medical speech data requires two fundamental technologies, i.e., automatic speech recognition to transcribe speech signals into text and named entity recognition to identify sensitive health information and its temporal location within the transcribed text. This study addresses both challenges in the context of bilingual medical audio containing English and Mandarin Chinese. First, we propose a multistage framework that employs language-specific ASR models with tailored training strategies based on data availability and quality. Second, we present an embedding–augmentation–labeling architecture that employs a large language model- based data augmentation technique to improve NER performance, particularly for underrepresented entity categories. Evaluated on the AICUP 2025 Medical Speech Sensitive Personal Data Recognition Competition dataset, the proposed method obtained a mixed error rate of 0.1299 and a macro F1-score of 0.6051, ultimately ranking third among 271 participating teams.

Keywords: Automatic Speech Recognition · Named Entity Recognition · Medical Speech Processing · Data Augmentation · Sensitive Health Information

1 Introduction

Processing information generated in medical settings is a key topic of concern in medical informatics [1], and speech streams or files constitute a major source of this information. Information, e.g., doctor–patient conversations, oral medical records by physicians, or recorded case discussions, are represented in the form of speech recordings. To perform semantic analyses of these speech recordings, most current technologies must convert the recording to text data, and automatic speech recognition (ASR) [2] technology can be employed to transcribe speech signals to text.

Numerous ASR models and commercial products have been developed; however, their applications to medical speech remain challenging. For example, a considerable

J. Jonnagaddala et al. (Eds.): IW-DMRN 2025, CCIS 2908, pp. 86–98, 2026.
https://doi.org/10.1007/978-981-92-2282-7_7

challenge is that medical speech contains several proper nouns, referred to as named entities, whose recognition requires extensive training with medical corpora. When general purpose ASR models are employed to process medical speech, these entities are more likely to be misrecognized than general nouns, thereby rendering the overall transcription unusable.

Even if medical speech can be successfully converted to a plain text format, the positions and categories of the named entities in the text must be labeled correctly, and this process is referred to as named entity recognition (NER) [3]. Typically, named entities play a crucial role in semantic analysis because they are the fundamental units of meaning within medical text. Consider the following example.

Albert Chen, a 45-year-old elementary school teacher, visited Dr. Chang today because he was not feeling well.

Here, the key information comprises the following elements: the patient is Albert Chen, he is an elementary school teacher, his age is 45, and his doctor is Dr. Chang. ASR errors can cause medical NER to fail. In turn, NER errors can negatively impact the accuracy of subsequent text analysis and applications. Such error accumulation can easily render the final recognition results of the entire system unusable. Thus, in the selection or design of models for each stage, downstream models must consider both accuracy and error tolerance toward upstream information. In addition, in privacy-sensitive contexts, accurately identifying when this information appears in the audio recording (temporal annotation) is crucial for downstream applications, e.g., automatic redaction or deidentification of sensitive portions of medical recordings.

These challenges are exemplified in the AICUP 2025 Medical Speech Sensitive Personal Data Recognition Competition [4], which focuses on automatically recognizing sensitive health information (SHI) in medical speech recordings. This competition requires systems to identify entity types and text spans, and provide precise temporal boundaries (i.e., timestamps) that indicate when each entity appears in the audio. This temporal dimension is critical for various applications, e.g., automatic redaction of sensitive information from medical recordings.

This study has two main objectives corresponding to the two competition tasks. First, for the speech transcription task, we propose a multistage system based on existing ASR models. By leveraging language-specific model selection and differentiated training strategies, this system is designed to improve transcription accuracy for bilingual medical audio. Second, for the NER task, we propose a system that combines word embedding models with a fully connected network and a conditional random field (CRF) [5] model to extract named entities from the text and label their categories with temporal boundaries.

1.1 Related Work

The AICUP 2025 Competition [4] addresses the dual challenge of ASR and temporal NER in medical speech. Unlike conventional NER tasks that only require identifying the entity spans in text, the AICUP 2025 Competition [6] requires systems to predict both the entity type and its precise temporal boundaries (i.e., the start and end timestamps) in the audio recording. This temporal dimension adds significant complexity because the systems must maintain accurate alignment between the transcribed text and the original audio signal. Previous work on speech-based deidentification has primarily focused on speaker anonymization, and systematic approaches to identifying and temporally locating SHI in medical speech remain underexplored [7]. Protecting sensitive health information in clinical data has been widely studied in the context of electronic health records (EHRs). De-identification methods aim to automatically detect and transform personally identifiable information to preserve patient privacy while maintaining the usability of the data. Chen et al. [8] proposed a surrogate generation approach for EHR de-identification, where sensitive entities are replaced with realistic surrogate values that retain the structural characteristics of the original text while removing identifiable information.

1.2 ASR

Diverse ASR architectures have been proposed in recent years. For example, Yao et al. [9] proposed a modified Conformer model called Zipformer, which implements the following improvements. (1) The middle stacks of U-Net-like encoders operate at lower frame rates, (2) more modules that reuse attention weights are incorporated to improve efficiency, (3) BiasNorm is utilized to preserve length information, (4) two new activation functions, i.e., SwooshR and SwooshL, are employed, and (5) the ScaledAdam optimizer is proposed and implemented. This optimizer achieves faster convergence and better performance than the conventional Adam optimizer.

Among these models, the most notable architecture is Whisper [10], which was proposed by OpenAI. The Whisper model is a standard encoder–decoder Transformer model. However, unlike most conventional ASR models that are strongly dependent on high-quality manually labeled speech datasets, the Whisper model is trained to predict transcripts from 680,000 h of largescale weakly supervised audio data collected from the Internet. In benchmark tests, the Whisper model has demonstrated accuracy that is comparable to that of fully supervised models under zero-shot transfer settings without the need for any fine-tuning processes. Distil-Whisper [11], which is a distilled version of the Whisper model, uses the word error rate to select the highest quality data from a largescale pseudo labeling dataset for model training. It distills the Whisper model into a variant with fewer parameters and faster inference, achieving accuracy comparable to that of the original model across multiple domains.

Several other studies have further developed and improved the Whisper model. For example, Bain et al. [12] proposed WhisperX, which incorporates voice activity detection and forced phoneme alignment. These two functions allow the WhisperX model to address inaccurate utterance timestamp alignment in long audio transcription, thereby reducing the errors observed in the conventional Whisper model, e.g., drifting, hallucination, and repetition. In addition, the Simul-Whisper model [13] leverages the time alignment embedded in the cross-attention mechanism of the Whisper model to guide autoregressive decoding, which enables chunk-based streaming ASR without fine-tuning the pretrained model. After evaluating both the accuracy and availability of ASR models, we selected the Whisper model as the ASR model for the proposed system architecture.

1.3 Medical NER

Many medical NER frameworks have been proposed in recent years. For example, Wu et al. [14] proposed a three-stage NER framework. In the first stage, this framework annotates and categorizes named entities in medical text using the model proposed by Ma et al. [15], which combines contextual and label semantics. In the second and third stages, a correction model is employed to address the tendency of end-to-end NER models to predict structurally incorrect labels while failing to recognize them [16].

In addition, Alamro et al. [17] proposed the BioBBC model, a biomedical NER (BioNER) model that utilizes a bidirectional encoder representations from Transformers (BERT)–bidirectional long short-term memory (BiLSTM)–CRF architecture and integrates multiple features. The embedding layer of this model generates enriched contextual representation vectors of the input through four types of embeddings, i.e., part-of-speech (POS) tag, char-level, BERT, and data specific embeddings. In addition, the BiLSTM layer produces additional syntactic and semantic feature representations, and the CRF layer identifies the best possible tag sequence for the input sentence.

The core of these studies is based on the fundamental embedding–augmentation–labeling architecture, which is well suited for sequence labeling tasks. Their differences lay in the types and quantity of the textual features embedded. Other studies have focused on fine-tuning pretrained models on medical text to improve the accuracy of the representation vectors generated via embeddings. For example, Gu et al. [18] proposed the PubMedBERT model, which is a language model pretrained from scratch on a large amount of unlabeled biomedical text data. Compared with language models that are initially trained on general domain text and then tuned, the PubMedBERT model realizes a significant performance improvement.

Furthermore, many medical NER models have begun to incorporate large language models (LLMs). For example, Keloth et al. [19] developed the BioNER–LLM meta AI (BioNER–LLaMA) model, which is tuned via instruction training. The instruction tuning framework in the BioNER–LLaMA model facilitates combining multiple available datasets and making modifications to only the prompts to extract specific or multiple types of entities. That study leveraged three existing annotated NER corpora with three different entity types, transforming them into instruction demonstrations and then combining the demonstrations to train a model that follows instruction. Evaluation results demonstrate that the BioNER–LLaMA model obtained strong performance across different NER datasets.

Wu et al. [20] proposed the PubMed Central–LLaMA model, which is an LLM specifically designed for medical applications. This model is fine-tuned using 4.8 million biomedical academic studies, 30,000 medical textbooks, and domain specific instructions. Note that the use of training samples was central to the current study; thus, we employed the embedding–augmentation–labeling architecture prevalent in previous studies, despite the strong performance of LLM-based NER methods.

Building on these advances in ASR and medical NER, the proposed method adapts state-of-the-art models to the specific challenges of bilingual medical speech with temporal annotation requirements. Previous studies have demonstrated the effectiveness of LLMs for medical NER in text [21]; however, the proposed method leverages

LLMs specifically for data augmentation rather than direct entity recognition, thereby addressing the data scarcity challenge inherent in SHI datasets.

2   Methodology

As shown in Fig. 1, the proposed method comprises two major modules, i.e., the ASR and NER modules. The ASR module comprises three steps: (1) data preprocessing using the UVR5 tool [22] to filter background noise, (2) language identification to determine whether the audio is Chinese or English, and (3) language-specific transcription to convert the speech to text and generate word-level timestamps. The design rationale for the language-specific processing is described in Section 3.1, and the model selection strategy is explained in Section 3.2.

The NER module comprises four steps, i.e., (1) text preprocessing to remove punctuation and manage abbreviations, (2) word embedding to convert each word into a representation vector using language-specific models, (3) dimensionality reduction using a fully connected neural network to produce token label vectors, and (4) sequence labeling using a CRF model to predict entity types with temporal boundaries. The data augmentation strategy employed to address class imbalance is described in Section 3.3.

2.1   Language Identification

Generally, ASR models obtain considerably better performance in domain-specific tasks if they are fine-tuned on domain-specific datasets. In previous studies, a prevalent approach to manage multilingual tasks is to employ a single multilingual model, which is advantageous because it can be trained on corpora from different languages simultaneously. In addition, this technique leverages transfer learning across languages, thereby enabling the ASR model to achieve satisfactory performance even for languages with limited resources.

However, we suggest using corresponding monolingual ASR models for different languages and employing different training strategies for certain conditions. For example, the dataset discussed in Section 4.1 contains both English and Chinese data, with the English data constituting the majority. The Chinese data constitute a much smaller proportion and contains some low-quality audio recordings. Trained on a dataset characterized by vast disparity in data volume and quality (where Chinese data are scarce and English data are abundant), the model tends to improve Chinese language recognition at the expense of its accuracy on English. Thus, rather than employing a single multilingual model, we utilize the corresponding monolingual ASR models for each language. In this case, all audio is first subjected to language identification, where a multilingual ASR model can be employed to detect the language. Using the Whisper model as an example, we set the language parameter to auto. If 50% or more of the first 10 tokens recognized by the Whisper model are Chinese words, then the audio file is classified as Chinese; otherwise, it is classified as English. We validated this approach on the AICUP 2025 training set, in which the audio files predominantly contain a single language with minimal code switching. This simple threshold-based method proved sufficient for the characteristics of the competition dataset.

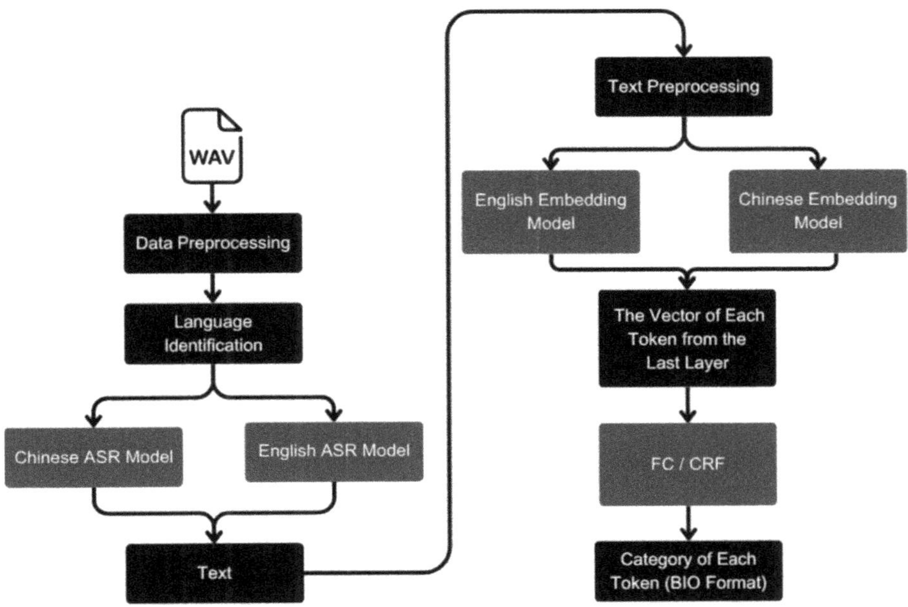

Fig. 1. Flow of proposed method. Audio is transcribed by language-specific ASR models, then processed via corresponding embeddings and an FC/CRF layer to output entity labels.

2.2 ASR Model

For the ASR model selection process, we adopted different strategies based on the characteristics of the training data. For English, the AICUP 2025 dataset provides 1,517 English audio files with approximately 10 h of high-quality professional recordings. With this substantial volume of domain-specific training data, we selected parakeet-tdt-0.6b-v2 [23] as the base model and fine-tuned it on the AICUP 2025 training data. The parakeet model is a lightweight Transformer-based ASR model that exhibits strong performance across various domains and can be fine-tuned efficiently.

For Chinese, the training set contains only 78 Chinese audio files with approximately 0.45 h of audio, some of which are extracted from television dramas and have variable recording quality. Performing fine-tuning processes on such limited data risks overfitting to noise patterns rather than learning robust speech representations. Thus, we employed the whisper-large-v3-turbo model [24] without any fine-tuning process, and we leveraged its extensive pretraining on diverse Chinese audio for better generalization.

This differentiated approach balances the tradeoffs between domain adaptation and overfitting risk based on the volume and quality of the available data.

2.3 Data Augmentation for NER Model

In NER training and test datasets, the volume of data for each category of named entities typically varies, with some categories having scarce data or no data. When trained on such datasets, the model tends to prioritize the overall performance by favoring the prediction of tokens into categories with a large volume of data while disregarding categories with scarce data. Thus, we propose a data augmentation technique that leverages an LLM to generate data.

First, after analyzing the volume of data for each category in the training dataset, the model selects several data entries from each of the categories with the scarcest data to serve as seed examples, thereby forming a seed pool. Then, the model randomly selects a single seed example from the seed pool and adds it to the LLM prompt in one shot, as an example. In addition, the primary instruction in the prompt is to "substantially reconstruct the structure, entity text, and semantic meaning of the example sentence while preserving the entity type." Requesting the LLM to generate multiple data entries simultaneously can result in overly similar data patterns; thus, the prompt of each example is designed to instruct the LLM to produce a single entry. Then, the generated data are added to the seed pool. This cycle of random selection, prompt synthesis, and data generation is repeated iteratively until the seed pool reaches the specified data volume.

2.4 Word-Level Labeling and Alignment

In this system, an ASR model first converts the speech data into text and outputs a timestamps for each word, indicating its start and end times in the audio, arranged as a linear sequence in speaking order. Then, an NER model takes exactly the same word sequence as input and predicts a single label for each word, e.g., B-type, I-type, or O. These labels follow the standard BIO (Beginning, Inside, Outside) tagging scheme. specifically, the 'B-type' tag marks the beginning of an entity span, the 'I-type' tag denotes tokens that are inside or continue the entity, and the 'O' tag is assigned to tokens that are outside of any entity. The word sequence input to the NER model is built directly from the ASR output after simple filtering and normalization. As a result, the first word, second word, and so on share the same index positions in both structures; thus, the system can align each NER label with its corresponding timestamps purely by index. When there is a run of labels starting with a B-type followed by one or more I- type of the same category, these words are merged into a single entity span whose start and end times are taken from the first word and last word in the span, respectively. Furthermore, if an isolated I-type label appears without a preceding B-type, that single word is treated as a one-word entity, and words labeled O are considered as non-entity background and are not output as entities.

2.5 Experiments

We validated the performance of the proposed framework in the AICUP 2025 Competition on Speech Privacy and Personal Information Recognition [1]. The dataset provided by AICUP 2025 is introduced in Section 4.1, and Section 4.2 describes the two metrics used in the performance evaluation. Section 4.3 explains the model types used in the proposed framework and the parameter settings used for model training, and Section 4.4 presents the performance metrics for the proposed framework on the ASR and NER tasks, as well as comparisons with those of other teams in the competition.

Dataset

SREDH-AICup SHI speech corpus 2025 dataset used in this study. The training dataset contained domestic (Taiwanese) and international sources, was employed in the experimental evaluations. The international portion comprises actual patient data from the Lowy Cancer Research Centre, University of New South Wales, Australia, which passed ethical review. These data were deidentified, transcribed, and then recorded by professional personnel. This English portion (referred to as ENG in Table 1) contains 1,517 audio files with a total duration of 10.058 h and 99,743 transcript words [25, 26].

As shown in Table 1, there is a significant imbalance in the distribution of named entity categories. High frequency categories, e.g., such as "Date," "Doctor," and "Duration" contain hundreds of instances. Conversely, many categories, including "Phone," "Fax," "Email," and various ID related fields, have few or no instances. This data scarcity for rare categories can hinder the model's ability to learn and generalize effectively. To mitigate this issue and improve the performance of the model, we implemented data augmentation techniques to enrich the training set for these underrepresented categories.

Table 1. Distribution of named entity categories in the AICUP 2025 training set (ENG = English training data; CHN = Chinese training data).

Categories	# in ENG	# in CHN	Categories	# in ENG	# in CHN
Patient	287	73	Date	1,129	30
Doctor	465	67	Time	264	14
User Name	0	0	Duration	479	7
Personal Name	227	5	Set	69	1
Family Name	154	17	Phone	2	0
Profession	39	3	Fax	0	0
Room	0	3	Email	0	0
Department	97	9	URL	1	0
Hospital	104	9	IP address	0	0
Organization	32	0	Other	0	0
Street	88	0	Social security number	0	0
City	116	3	Medical record number	99	0
State	104	0	Health plan number	0	0
Country	14	0	Account number	0	0
County	4	0	License number	0	0
Zip	82	0	Vehicle ID	0	0
Location-Other	15	0	Device ID	0	0
District	1	0	Biometric ID	0	0
Age	49	7	ID number	235	0

The domestic (Taiwanese) portion includes online medical educational videos and authorized audio segments from medical video content. This Chinese portion (CHN in Table 1) contains 78 audio files with a total duration of 0.446 h and 5,379 transcript words.

The dataset includes a named entity annotation file. Each entry contains the name, category, and timestamp of a named entity in a particular audio file. A total of 38 named entities were available. Table 1 shows the categories of named entities in the training dataset and the number of named entities in each category. The English test dataset contained 639 audio files totaling 4.560 h, and the Chinese test dataset contained 71 audio files totaling 0.440 h. Note that the test data do not include the above-mentioned transcripts and marked files.

In addition, the competition organizers provided separate validation and test sets; however, only the test set results are used for final evaluation.

Evaluation Methods and Metrics

We output a transcript and a named entity annotation file for each audio file in the test dataset and then submitted them to AICUP 2025 for performance evaluation. Here, the ASR performance was evaluated in terms of the mixed error rate (MER), which is calculated as follows:

$$MER = \frac{S + D + N}{N} \tag{1}$$

where N, S, D, and I denote the total number of words in the ground truth transcript, the number of substituted words (i.e., the words in the ground truth that the model replaced with different words), the number of deleted words (i.e., words present in the ground truth transcript but missing in the model output), and the number of inserted words (i.e., words in the model output that are not present in the ground truth transcript), respectively.

To evaluate the NER performance, we used the macro F1-score, which is calculated as follows.

$$macro\ F1 - score = \frac{2}{N} \sum_{i=0}^{N} \frac{Precision_i \times Recall_i}{Precision_i + Recall_i} \tag{2}$$

For NER evaluation, the competition utilizes temporal overlap-based metrics. Here, an entity prediction is considered correct only if (1) the entity type matches the ground truth and (2) the predicted temporal boundaries overlap with the ground truth times-tamps. The precision and recall for each category are calculated based on the duration of the temporal overlap between the predicted and ground truth entities. Note that partial matches contribute proportionally based on their overlap duration. Readers can refer to the competition documentation [1] for the detailed definitions of TP, FP, and FN in this temporal framework.

Model Parameter Settings

The models used in this study included whisper-large-v3-turbo [19] for language identification, parakeet-tdt-0.6b-v2 [18] for English-language ASR, whisper-large-v3-turbo [19] for Chinese-language ASR, mdeberta-v3-base for Chinese word embedding,

DeBERTa-v3-large for English word embedding, and Gemini (i.e., a data-generation model) for data augmentation.

For the English ASR, we fine-tuned the parakeet-tdt-0.6b-v2 model on the AICUP 2025 English training data using the model's default training configuration with a learning rate of 1e−4 and 50 epochs. For the Chinese ASR, we employed the whisper-largev3-turbo model in zero-shot mode without fine-tuning.

The parameters used to train the Chinese and English word embedding models in the NER task were as follows: batch size = 8, weight decay = 1e−2, lr scheduler type = "cosine," learning rate = 2e−5, number of training epochs = 8, and Bf16 = True.

3 Results

Table 2 shows the performance of the proposed method and the top-performing and 30th-ranked models in AICUP 2025 on the ASR and NER tasks. As can be seen, the proposed method obtained an MER value and macro F1-score of 0.1299 and 0.6051, respectively, which are comparable to the best results and significantly surpassed those of the 30th-ranked model. Considering both the ASR and NER performance in AICUP 2025, the proposed method ranked third among all participating teams in terms of overall performance. Note that AICUP 2025 did not provide detailed test results; thus, we could not perform an error analysis.

Table 2. Performance comparison on AICUP 2025 test set.

	Top performing team	Proposed method	Rank 30
MER (lower is better)	0.1147	0.1299	0.2115
macro F1-score (higher is better)	0.7103	0.6051	0.2079

4 Discussion

The proposed framework achieved an MER of 0.1299 and a macro F1-score of 0.6051, ranking third among 271 teams in the AICUP 2025 competition. These results validate the core design choices while also revealing where further gains are possible. Two aspects of the system are worth examining more closely: the language-specific ASR strategy and the LLM-driven data augmentation for NER.

The decision to use separate monolingual ASR models rather than a single multilingual system was driven by the severe data imbalance between the English (1,517 files, ~10 h) and Chinese (78 files, ~0.45 h) training sets. A joint model trained on such disparate volumes tends to sacrifice performance on the minority language. Applying whisper-large-v3-turbo [24] in zero-shot mode for Chinese avoided overfitting to low-quality recordings, leveraging the model's extensive pretraining on diverse audio as described in Radford et al. [10]. For English, fine-tuning parakeet-tdt-0.6b-v2 [23] on domain-specific data followed the well-established principle that adaptation to target-domain speech yields consistent gains when sufficient data are available [9, 11]. The small MER gap between the proposed method (0.1299) and the top team (0.1147) likely reflects the continued difficulty of low-resource Chinese transcription rather than any fundamental weakness in the English pipeline.

On the NER side, the primary challenge was the highly imbalanced entity distribution shown in Table 1. Categories such as "Date" and "Doctor" contained hundreds of training instances, whereas "Fax," "Email," and several identifier types had none at all. Without intervention, embedding-based sequence labelers tend to collapse predictions toward frequent categories. The iterative LLM augmentation strategy—sampling seed examples from underrepresented categories and prompting the model to reconstruct semantically varied instances—directly addresses this. Compared to instruction-tuned models like BioNER-LLaMA [19], which use LLMs for direct entity inference, the present approach restricts LLM involvement to data generation, keeping the downstream DeBERTa-CRF architecture lightweight. The CRF layer, as in BioBBC [17], remains essential for enforcing globally valid BIO tag sequences, which is particularly important given the temporal annotation requirement of the competition [4, 6].

The temporal overlap evaluation metric adds a layer of difficulty not present in standard NER benchmarks: a correctly identified entity type still incurs a penalty if the predicted timestamps do not align with ground truth. This makes the system sensitive to upstream ASR errors—substitutions or deletions shift word indices and, consequently, misalign the NER labels with their audio positions. This cascading error problem has been observed in pipeline-based NER systems [14] and is amplified here by the strict temporal scoring. Approaches like WhisperX [12], which refine timestamp accuracy through forced phoneme alignment, could help reduce such mismatches in future iterations.

Situating this work in the wider field of clinical de-identification, speech-based SHI recognition remains considerably less explored than its text-based counterpart [7]. Most prior de-identification research has focused on EHR text [1, 8], and datasets enabling temporal evaluation over speech are rare—the SREDH-AICup corpus [25, 26] being one notable exception. The macro F1-score of 0.6051, far above the 30th-ranked team's 0.2079, suggests that the combination of domain-adapted

ASR and augmentation-assisted NER represents a practically useful baseline for this task. Closing the remaining gap to the top-performing team will likely require richer multifeature embeddings, incorporating character-level or POS-tag representations [17], and more targeted handling of zero-instance entity categories.

5   Conclusion

This paper has proposed a robust multistage framework designed to address the challenges of the ASR and NER tasks in bilingual medical audio environments. The contributions and experimental results are summarized as follows.Strategic ASR for Mixed-language Data. We implemented a tailored ASR strategy that can handle English and Chinese medical speech. LLM-driven Data Augmentation. To overcome the scarcity of high-quality annotated medical data, we leveraged LLMs to correct typographical errors and generate augmented training samples. This approach significantly increased the volume of training data while maintaining strict quality guarantees, thereby directly contributing to improved NER accuracy. Performance Validation. The effectiveness of the proposed framework was validatedthrough the AICUP 2025 competition. The proposed method achieved an F1-score of 0.6051, achieving third place among the 271 teams that participated in the competition.These results are promising; however, several avenues should be considered for further investigation to fully characterize the potential of the proposed framework. Future work will focus on the following areas. Ablation Studies. We plan to perform a comprehensive ablation study to quantify the individual contributions of each stage in the proposed framework. This will clarify how different models and processing steps specifically affect overall perform Multifeature Integration: Currently, our model relies primarily on semantic textual embeddings. Following the success observed in recent studies, we plan to incorporate multifeature representation vectors, e.g., POS tags or character-level embeddings, to capture finer grammatical and morphological nuances, potentially boosting NER precision.Generalizability Testing. To verify the robustness of the proposed method beyond the specific context of the AICUP 2025 dataset, we plan to validate the framework on diverse public medical audio benchmarks and real-world clinical datasets.

Acknowledgments. This work was supported by the Ministry of Education and the National Science and Technology Council under grant NSTC 113-2410-H-992-006-MY3.

Disclosure of Interests. The authors declare that they have no competing interests relevant to the content of this article.

References

1. Jonnagaddala, J., Wong, Z.S.-Y.: Privacy preserving strategies for electronic health records in the era of large language models. Npj Digit. Med. **8**(1), 34 (2025)
2. Yu, D., Deng, L.: Automatic Speech Recognition, vol. 1. Springer (2016)
3. Nadeau, D., Sekine, S.: A survey of named entity recognition and classification. Lingvisticae Investigationes. **30**(1), 3–26 (2007)
4. Codabench. AICUP *2025* Competition on Speech Privacy and Personal Information Recognition. (2025). Available from: https://www.codabench.org/competitions/4890.
5. Lafferty, J., A. McCallum, F.C. Pereira: Conditional random fields: Probabilistic models for segmenting and labeling sequence data. 2001.
6. Dai, H.-J., et al.: Leveraging State-of-the-Art LLMs for the De-identification of Sensitive Health Information in Clinical Speech. medRxiv: p. 2026.04.13.26349911 (2026).
7. Dai, H.-J., et al.: Leveraging large language models for the deidentification and temporal normalization of sensitive health information in electronic health records. Npj Digit. Med. **8**(1), 517 (2025)
8. Chen, A., et al.: Generation of surrogates for De-identification of electronic health records. Stud. Health Technol. Inform. **264**, 70–73 (2019)
9. Yao, Z., et al.: Zipformer: A faster and better encoder for automatic speech recognition. arXiv preprint https://arxiv.org/abs/2310.11230, (2023).
10. Radford, A., et al.: Robust speech recognition via large-scale weak supervision. in International conference on machine learning. 2023. PMLR.
11. Gandhi, S., P. Von Platen, A.M. Rush, Distil-whisper: Robust knowledge distillation via large-scale pseudo labelling. arXiv preprint https://arxiv.org/abs/2311.00430, 2023.
12. Bain, M., et al.: *Whisperx: Time-accurate speech transcription of long-form audio.* arXiv preprint https://arxiv.org/abs/2303.00747, (2023).

13. Wang, H., et al.: *Simul-whisper: Attention-guided streaming whisper with truncation detection.* arXiv preprint https://arxiv.org/abs/2406.10052, (2024).
14. Wu, J.-J., Chang, T.-H., Hsu, F.-Y.: ISLab at ROCLING 2023 MultiNER-health task: a three-stage NER model combining textual content and tagged semantics. In: Proceedings of the 35th Conference on Computational Linguistics and Speech Processing (ROCLING 2023) (2023)
15. Ma, J., et al. Label semantics for few shot named entity recognition. in Findings of the association for computational linguistics: ACL 2022. (2022).
16. Lin, B.-S., Chen, J.-H., Chang, T.-H.: NERVE at ROCLING 2022 shared task: a comparison of three named entity recognition frameworks based on language model and lexicon approach. In: Proceedings of the 34th Conference on Computational Linguistics and Speech Processing (ROCLING 2022) (2022)
17. Alamro, H., et al.: BioBBC: a multi-feature model that enhances the detection of biomedical entities. Sci. Rep. **14**(1), 7697 (2024)
18. Gu, Y., et al.: Domain-specific language model pretraining for biomedical natural language processing. ACM Trans. Comput. Healthc. (HEALTH). **3**(1), 1–23 (2021)
19. Keloth, V.K., et al.: Advancing entity recognition in biomedicine via instruction tuning of large language models. Bioinformatics. **40**(4), btae163 (2024)
20. Wu, C., et al.: PMC-LLaMA: toward building open-source language models for medicine. J. Am. Med. Inform. Assoc. **31**(9), 1833–1843 (2024)
21. Panchal, O., et al.:Benchmarking Large Language Models for De-identification of Electronic Health Record Notes. 2026.
22. Github. Ultimate Vocal Remover GUI. (2025.); Available from: https://github.com/Anjok07/ultimatevocalremovergui.
23. NVIDIA. *Hugging Face.* (2025.); Available from: https://huggingface.co/nvidia/para-keet-tdt-0.6b-v.
24. OpenAI, Hugging *Face.* (2024).
25. Jonnagaddala, J., et al.: The OpenDeID corpus for patient de-identification. Sci. Rep. **11**(1), 19973 (2021)
26. Dai, H.J., et al.: A Clinical Speech Corpus with Temporally Aligned Sensitive Health Information (2026). https://www.medrxiv.org/content/10.64898/2026.03.31.26349906v2

Speech De-identification of Chinese, English and Minnan: Effectiveness of Chinese-based LLM Model and ASR

Yuan-Chi Hsu[1,2]([✉]) [iD] and Hong-Jie Dai[1,2,3,4] [iD]

[1] Intelligent System Laboratory, Department of Electrical Engineering, College of Electrical Engineering and Computer Science, National Kaohsiung University of Science and Technology, Kaohsiung, Taiwan
asm1478406@gmail.com, hjdai@nkust.edu.tw
[2] National Institute of Cancer Research, National Health Research Institutes, Tainan, Taiwan
[3] School of Post-Baccalaureate Medicine, College of Medicine, Kaohsiung Medical University, Kaohsiung, Taiwan
[4] Center for Big Data Research, Kaohsiung Medical University, Kaohsiung, Taiwan

Abstract. This study addresses the critical challenge of privacy preservation in multilingual clinical environments, specifically targeting English, Mandarin Chinese, and Minnan. We propose a robust automatic de-identification framework that integrates a multilingual pre-trained Automatic Speech Recognition model with Large Language Models to accurately transcribe and redact sensitive patient information. A key contribution of this work is the evaluation of efficient fine-tuning strategies; we demonstrate that a partial fine-tuning approach - focusing on specific model layers with limited domain-specific data—substantially enhances performance compared to full-parameter training. To overcome challenges inherent in code-switching and mixed-script scenarios, the system employs a hybrid recognition mechanism combining dictionary-based matching, regular expressions, and Large Language Models -based reasoning. Experimental evaluations validate the efficacy of this approach, where the optimized model achieved a Word Error Rate of 7.86% and a Character Error Rate of 4.17% in mixed-language tasks. These findings confirm that the proposed method provides a scalable and accurate solution for de-identifying medical speech, facilitating the secondary use of clinical data for research while ensuring strict patient privacy.

Keywords: Medical speech de-identification · Automatic speech recognition · Large language models · Sensitive health information

1 Introduction

This study investigates automated methods for identifying and de-identifying sensitive personal information in medical speech data, focusing on multilingual scenarios that reflect real-world clinical settings in Taiwan and internationally. The dataset includes utterances in Chinese, English, and Minnan, capturing the linguistic diversity commonly found in healthcare communications. However, the overall data volume

J. Jonnagaddala et al. (Eds.): IW-DMRN 2025, CCIS 2908, pp. 99–111, 2026.
https://doi.org/10.1007/978-981-92-2282-7_8

remains relatively limited, particularly for Minnan and domain-specific expressions, posing challenges for robust model training and generalization.

Recent work has demonstrated that large language models can effectively identify and normalize protected health information in electronic health records. For example, Dai et al. [2] showed that LLM-based systems can achieve strong performance in clinical de-identification tasks while also supporting temporal normalization of sensitive information in medical narratives. These results highlight the growing potential of Large Language Models (LLMs) as scalable tools for automated privacy protection in healthcare data.

In automated clinical de-identification pipelines [3], sensitive identifiers detected in electronic health records are often replaced with realistic surrogate values rather than simply removed, allowing the resulting text to preserve its structure and contextual coherence for downstream analysis. Algorithms for generating such surrogates have been proposed to create plausible replacements that maintain the statistical and linguistic properties of the original clinical documents while protecting patient privacy [4].

The core task addressed in this work is the precise extraction of speech segments containing sensitive information such as personal names, dates, addresses, and institution names. Extending the text-centric objectives of the 2023 SREDH/AI-Cup Competition [5], which focused on the de-identification and temporal normalization of EHR notes, to the acoustic domain, this work is critical for downstream privacy-preserving applications in clinical NLP and facilitates the secondary use of speech data for research, training, and automated documentation systems. To this end, we examine the effectiveness of fine-tuning the *Whisper-Large-v3* model [6], originally adapted for Mandarin, with a limited set of additional multilingual data. Specifically, we evaluate whether such fine-tuning can outperform the base, non-fine-tuned model in identifying sensitive content across diverse language inputs, particularly under low-resource conditions. This study aims to provide insights into cross-lingual adaptation strategies for Automatic Speech Recognition (ASR)-based de-identification in mixed-language medical speech.

The growing adoption of large language models for clinical text analysis has also raised significant concerns regarding patient privacy and regulatory compliance. Recent studies highlight that sensitive health information contained in electronic health records must be protected through techniques such as de-identification, surrogate generation, and other privacy-preserving strategies when deploying AI systems in healthcare environments [7].

2 Data Processing

The dataset exhibits a substantial imbalance in language distribution, with English samples vastly outnumbering their Chinese counterparts (2263,78, see Fig. 1). Minnan expressed in Chinese script, is severely underrepresented. Such disparity in resource availability may hinder the model's ability to generalize to low-resource languages, potentially degrading overall recognition performance.

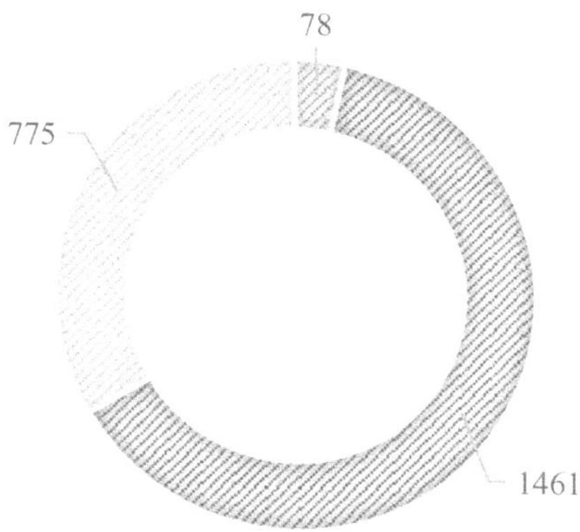

Fig. 1. Proportion of Chinese and English datasets.

Since the original *BELLE-2/Belle-Whisper-Large-v3-zh* [8] model was trained primarily on Simplified Chinese text, all training data in this study were first converted from Traditional to Simplified Chinese using OpenCC [9]. Although the original dataset was also normalized with whisper-normalizer, issues arose with the package's default behavior (such as converting '0' to 'O'). Therefore, a custom normalization process was adopted, which involved removing all punctuation, trimming leading and trailing whitespace, and converting text to lowercase.

The two sets of annotated data were reformatted into a JSON structure, where each sentence was treated as a property and all corresponding labels were stored as array attributes within the same object. This design facilitates efficient extraction and learning for large language models.

Regarding the extraction of time segments, the fine-tuned Belle model could not be directly applied in WhisperX for timestamp alignment. To address this, the CTranslate library [10] was used for model conversion. Although some degradation in Word Error Rate (WER)/ Character Error Rate (CER) metrics was observed during this process, preserving temporal information was prioritized. Additionally, since the timestamps generated by WhisperX were limited to the character level and could not accurately match multi-character words, a smoothing strategy and fuzzy matching mechanism were implemented to improve the robustness and accuracy of entity extraction, even in the presence of minor recognition errors.

In the dataset utilized for this study, the distribution of annotation labels was found to be highly imbalanced. Fig. 2 presents the statistical breakdown of label occurrences in both the training and validation sets. After further dividing these labels by language type (Chinese and English), the number of samples for certain categories decreased even further, exacerbating the data sparsity issue. To address the lack of representation of low-resource categories during model training, we employed a **dictionary-based augmentation strategy** during the data preprocessing stage, expanding the annotation set by incorporating frequently occurring sensitive entities such as occupations and place names. This approach aimed at enhancing the model's ability to identify these types of information.

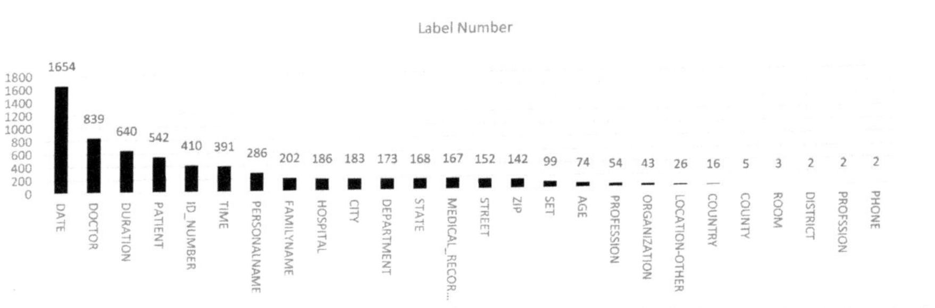

Fig. 2. Dataset label ratio.

3   Methods

3.1   Dataset

This study utilizes the **SREDH-AICup SHI speech corpus 2025 which is constructed from OpenDeID v2 corpus** provided by Secure Research Environment for Digital Health (SREDH) and used in the SREDH/AI-Cup competition for evaluating automated de-identification systems on electronic health records [1]. The dataset contains **2,100 pathology reports from 1,833 patients**, primarily related to cancer pathology, with an average length of approximately **700 tokens per report**. In total, the corpus includes **38,414 manually annotated protected health information (PHI) entities** across multiple sensitive categories [11]. All identifiers are replaced with surrogate values to preserve privacy while maintaining the linguistic structure of clinical text. The dataset demonstrates **high annotation reliability (inter-annotator agreement > 0.94)** and serves as a benchmark resource for evaluating machine learning and large language model approaches for clinical de-identification.

3.2 Model Selection and Rationale

In this study, we selected *Whisper-Large-v3* as the ASR backbone due to its strong multilingual generalization ability and robustness in low-resource and code-switched settings. Compared to Wav2Vec2 model, which often require separate fine-tuned models for each language, Whisper demonstrates better zero-shot performance on underrepresented languages such as Minnan, while maintaining acceptable accuracy on Chinese and English. Its unified architecture simplifies the pipeline and facilitates cross-lingual modeling.

As large language models continue to evolve rapidly, benchmarking is necessary to systematically evaluate and compare their performance across tasks and datasets. Standardized benchmarks provide a consistent framework for measuring model capabilities and identifying strengths and limitations, helping determine the suitability of different models for specific applications such as clinical information processing [12].

For the post-ASR de-identification task, we employed instruction-tuned LLMs such as Qwen3 [13]. These models allow for prompt-based entity extraction, which is particularly effective in settings with limited labeled data. By leveraging external dictionaries and descriptive prompts, the LLMs can compensate for insufficient Chinese training data, especially for proper nouns and domain-specific terms. This combination enhances the system's ability to generalize from a small set of annotated Chinese examples. Overall, the integration of Whisper and LLMs offers a practical and scalable solution for multilingual de-identification, especially under data-constrained clinical conditions.

This study adopts the Belle model, developed by Be Everyone's LLM Engine (BELLE). This model is fine-tuned based on *Whisper-Large-v3*, utilizing various open-source Chinese speech corpora, including AISHELL-1, AISHELL-2, Wenetspeech Net, Wenetspeech Meeting, and HKUST Dev. The fine-tuning process for Belle is detailed on its GitHub page [14]. During training, the model applies random masking along the temporal axis of the speech spectrogram and introduces noise simulation to enhance the diversity of the data, thereby improving recognition performance and generalization ability. Table 1 presents the evaluation scores of this model on various datasets for reference.

Table 1. Performance Comparison of Three Models as Reported in the Original. Belle Paper

Model	aishell_1	aishell_2	wenetspeech_net	wenetspeech_meeting	HKUST_dev
whisper-large-v3	8.085	5.475	11.72	20.15	28.597
Belle-whisper-large-v2-zh	2.549	3.746	8.503	14.598	16.289
Belle-whisper-large-v3-zh	2.781	3.786	8.865	11.246	16.440

3.3 System Implementation and Model Fine-tuning Details

During the model fine-tuning stage, we observed that fine-tuning the last 20 layers of BELLE yielded superior performance. Consequently, this configuration was adopted as the primary setting in this study. Throughout the research process, we also experimented with combining the outputs of both Whisper and BELLE models, employing a LLM to select or merge results through multiple-choice strategies. However, experimental results showed that this approach did not outperform the BELLE model alone and was ultimately abandoned.

During the training of the BELLE model, several advanced techniques were employed, including learning rate warmup, mixed precision training, and early stopping. Learning rate warmup helps to stabilize training in the initial stages by gradually increasing the learning rate, which can prevent divergence and facilitate better convergence, especially when using large-scale models and datasets. Mixed precision training reduces memory usage and accelerates computation by leveraging both 16-bit and 32-bit floating-point operations without significant loss in accuracy. Early stopping serves as an effective regularization strategy by halting training when the validation performance ceases to improve, thereby reducing the risk of overfitting and ensuring better generalization to unseen data. Detailed hyperparameters and training configurations are summarized in Table 2.

Table 2. BELLE training parameters.

Parameter	Setting
learning_rate	1e-5
warmup_steps	100
early_stopping	5
fp16	True
optim	adamw_bnb_8bit

Since the dataset contains Chinese text, we selected Qwen3-4B, developed by the Qwen team, as the default large language model. In this version, Qwen3-4B introduces a "Thinking Mode" and significantly expands its training corpus to 36 trillion tokens twice as many as version 2.5 and supports up to 100 languages. The model architecture consists of 36 layers, with 32 query attention heads (Q) and 8 key/value attention heads (KV). Its native context length supports 32,768 tokens and can be extended to 131,072 tokens using YaRN technology. However, considering the limited text length in this study, the extended context feature was not utilized. In addition, Qwen3-4B natively incorporates the ROLA [15] technique, with listing the ROLA parameter settings adopted in this study.

Since the base model alone occupies more than 10 GB of memory, parameter-efficient fine-tuning [14] was employed in this study, combined with LoRA and mixed precision training, to enable larger batch sizes and accelerate the overall training process. PEFT allows only a subset of parameters to be updated during fine-tuning, greatly reducing computational and memory requirements while maintaining performance comparable to full-parameter fine-tuning. Additionally, to further enhance training speed and resource utilization, the BitsAndBytes (BNB) quantization mechanism was adopted using the QLoRA [16] approach. QLoRA applies 4-bit quantization to compress model weights significantly, lowering memory consumption and enabling efficient fine-tuning of large models even on limited hardware resources. The corpus was not subject to special preprocessing, allowing Qwen-4B to directly learn the annotation standards of human annotators. Table 3 and Table 4 list detailed hyperparameter settings.

Table 3. Qwen3 Lora Parameters

Parameter	Setting
LoRA rank	64
lora_alpha	128
lora_dropout	0.1
target_modules	q_proj, k_proj, v_proj, o_proj, gate_proj, up_proj, down_proj
task_type	CAUSAL_LM

Table 4. Qwne training Parameters

Parameter	Setting
learning_rate	1e-4
early_stopping	3
fp16	True
optim	paged_adamw_8bit

Figure. 3 presents the three approaches employed to extract sensitive information from text: dictionary-based matching, regular expressions (Regex), and LLMs. The dictionary was constructed by incorporating labels identified in previous datasets. Given the limited manual annotations for Chinese, additional relevant labels were expanded using GPT-based augmentation. During data integration, rigorous duplicate filtering was applied, along with priority rules for instances where the same word was assigned multiple labels. When words overlapped, the longer word was given priority. Superfluous terms, such as prefixes like "Dr." in "Dr. Allen," were also removed.

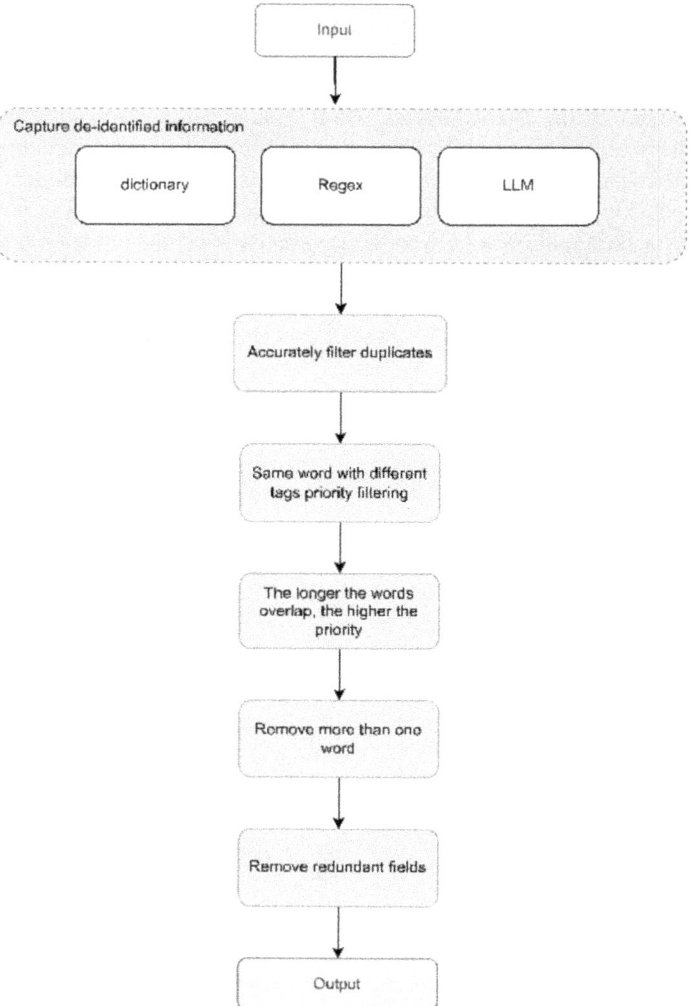

Fig. 3. Overall System Workflow.

4   Evaluation Metrics

In ASR evaluation, Match Error Rate (MER) is a widely adopted metric for quantifying the discrepancy between model predictions and reference transcriptions. It is calculated as follows:

$$\text{MER} = \frac{S + D + I}{N},$$

where S denotes the number of substitutions, D the number of deletions, I the number of insertions, and N the total number of words in the reference transcript. A lower MER indicates higher accuracy in the recognition results.

In text-based annotation tasks such as the identification of sensitive entities in clinical notes, the F1-score is commonly used to assess overall detection performance. The F1-score integrates both Precision and Recall, and is defined as:

$$\text{Precision} = \frac{\text{True Positive}}{\text{True Positive} + \text{False Positive}},$$

$$\text{Recall} = \frac{\text{True Positive}}{\text{True Positive} + \text{False Negative}},$$

$$\text{F1} - \text{score} = 2 \times \frac{\text{Precision} \times \text{Recall}}{\text{Precision} + \text{Recall}}.$$

In the context of segment-level annotation, predicted segments that overlap with annotated segments are counted as True Positives, annotated segments not detected are False Negatives, and predicted segments not matching any annotation are False Positives. The F1-score thus effectively captures both the accuracy and completeness of sequence detection in time-aligned annotation tasks

5   Results

Table 5 shows the comparison between the original (unfine-tuned) *Whisper-Large-v3* and BELLE models. As shown in Fig. 4, the unfine-tuned BELLE model exhibits a pronounced bias towards outputting Chinese text, regardless of the input language. However, this issue is effectively resolved after fine-tuning (Fig. 5). In addition, we performed a comparative analysis of the final competition audio samples in Chinese. The results reveal that, although the fine-tuned v3 model still displays some stuttering or disfluency when recognizing Chinese, the fine-tuned Belle model can maintain fluent and accurate Chinese transcription, preserving the strengths of the original model in handling Mandarin speech.

Table 5. Comparison of Original Models

Model	Whisper	BELLE
WER	10.14%	55.76%
CER	4.81%	59.09%

Reference: the lab report for tomas s case linked to lab no 6 x 93654
Predict: 這一實驗報告是湯姆斯的案件與所及至令六九六五三四

Fig. 4. Performance of the Belle model without fine-tuning on speech examples.

```
Reference: the lab report for tomas s case linked to lab no 6 x 93654
Predict: the lab report for thomas s case linked to lab number 6 x 93654
```

Fig. 5. Performance of the Belle model after fine-tuning on speech examples.

In this study, we fine-tuned only the last 20 decoder layers of the BELLE model. This approach preserves pre-trained acoustic features while enabling effective adaptation to the task-specific domain, particularly given the limited dataset size. Table 6 shows BELLE outperforms other strategies: pretrained on large-scale Mandarin corpora, it stabilized quickly despite initial English misrecognitions and demonstrated greater adaptability and stability than Whisper-Large-v3.

Table 6. Training Mixed Chinese and English performance

Model	Whisper (Only train the last 20 layers)	BELLE (Only train the last 20 layers)	BELLE (fine-tune)
WER	9.31%	**7.86%**	8.51%
CER	4.44%	**4.17%**	4.23%

Given the extreme imbalance in our dataset (Chinese to English ratio of 1:0.034), we investigated BELLE's fine-tuning performance on the limited English portion. Table 7 shows that full-parameter fine-tuning outperformed the Whisper baseline, demonstrating that a Mandarin-pretrained model can adapt cross-lingually. Fine-tuning only the last 20 encoder layers was less effective, suggesting that full-parameter updates may be more suitable in extremely low-resource scenarios.

Table 7. Only Training English performance

Model	Whisper (fine-tune)	BELLE (fine-tune)	Whisper (Only train the last 20 layers)	BELLE (Only train the last 20 layers)
WER	8.74%	**8.09%**	9.98%	8.58%
CER	4.30%	4.36%	4.71%	**4.24%**

6 Discussion

6.1 Language Imbalance and Generalization Performance

Models trained predominantly on English data tend to favor English syntactic and phonetic patterns, reducing recognition accuracy for Chinese or Minnan content. Structural differences such as the lack of explicit word boundaries in Chinese, greater reliance on context, and flexible word order, make Chinese entity recognition more prone to mis-segmentation and misclassification. Additionally, the scarcity of training samples limits the model's ability to reliably identify sensitive entities in Chinese. To mitigate the limitations posed by the low availability of Chinese resources, a dictionary-based augmentation strategy was employed. Specifically, domain-specific dictionaries containing common names, medical terms, locations, and time-related expressions were integrated into the post-processing pipeline. These dictionaries served as supplementary knowledge, enabling the system to compensate for missing or poorly learned representations by matching substrings in the ASR output with known sensitive terms. This hybrid approach of leveraging external linguistic knowledge partially alleviates the drawbacks of resource imbalance and enhances entity recall in Chinese and Minnan utterances.

While this study demonstrates the efficacy of the Whisper framework, we acknowledge the potential evaluation bias introduced by the dataset imbalance. The predominance of Mandarin and English segments compared to Taiwanese Hokkien may skew aggregate performance metrics (e.g., overall F1-score). Consequently, the reported high performance might disproportionately reflect the model's proficiency in high-resource languages, potentially masking performance degradation in low-resource linguistic segments. Future work will incorporate stratified evaluation metrics to isolate and assess performance across balanced subsets of each language to mitigate this bias.

7 Conclusion

This study presents a cross-lingual de-identification framework for medical speech data that integrates ASR and LLMs, validated on a multilingual dataset (Mandarin Chinese, English, and Taiwanese Hokkien). Through systematic experiments, we evaluated the impact of various data sources and fine-tuning strategies on sensitive information identification. Results show that, after initial fine-tuning on Mandarin, even a small amount of domain-specific multilingual data significantly improves de-identification performance compared to using the base model or a single-language fine-tuned model. The proposed approach, incorporating diverse annotation strategies and robust post-processing procedures (e.g., overlap filtering and fuzzy matching), further enhances accuracy and robustness. Importantly, the framework maintains strong performance under limited annotated data, highlighting its potential for real-world clinical data privacy protection and downstream medical AI applications. Future work may extend this framework to additional languages and more complex medical speech contexts, exploring the feasibility and limitations of speech de-identification in specialized clinical domains.

Acknowledgments. This study was supported in part by the National Institute of Cancer Research, National Health Research Institutes, Tainan, Taiwan, and the Center for Big Data Research at Kaohsiung Medical University. The authors would like to thank the organizers of the AI CUP 2025 Spring competition for providing the dataset and the evaluation platform that made this research possible.

Disclosure of Interests. The authors have no competing interests to declare that are relevant to the content of this article.

Appendix A. Prompt Templates

Extract sensitive health information entities from the following medical dialogue.

Target Entity Categories:
- PATIENT: Patient names
- DOCTOR: Doctor names
- FAMILYNAME: Family member names
- PERSONALNAME: Personal names (not patient/doctor)
- PROFESSION: Job titles or professions
- DEPARTMENT: Hospital departments
- HOSPITAL: Hospital or clinic names
- ORGANIZATION: Organizations or institutions
- STREET/CITY/DISTRICT/COUNTY/STATE/COUNTRY/ZIP: Location information
- LOCATION-OTHER: Other location references
- AGE: Age information
- DATE/TIME/DURATION/SET: Temporal information
- MEDICAL_RECORD_NUMBER/ID_NUMBER: Identification numbers
Instructions:
1. Identify ALL entities that match the categories above
2. Extract exact text spans as they appear
3. Return ONLY entities present in the text
4. Use exact category names from the list above
Output format:
{"entities": [{"text": "<entity_text>", "category": "<entity_category>"}]}
Input: "Hello Dr. Chen, I am 65-year-old patient John Wang, here for a follow-up at Zhongshan Hospital Cardiology Department today."
Output: {"entities": [{"text": "Dr. Chen", "category": "PROFESSION"}, {"text": "65", "category": "AGE"}, {"text": "John Wang", "category": "PATIENT"}, {"text": "Zhongshan Hospital", "category": "HOSPITAL"}, {"text": "Cardiology Department", "category": "DEPARTMENT"}]}
Input: "{line["text"]}"
Output:

References

1. Dai, H.J., et al.: A Clinical Speech Corpus with Temporally Aligned Sensitive Health Information (2026). https://www.medrxiv.org/content/10.64898/2026.03.31.26349906v2
2. Dai, H.-J., et al.: Leveraging large language models for the deidentification and temporal normalization of sensitive health information in electronic health records. npj Digit. Med. **8**(1), 517 (2025)
3. Dai, H.-J., et al.: Leveraging State-of-the-Art LLMs for the De-identification of Sensitive Health Information in Clinical Speech. medRxiv, p. 2026.04.13.26349911 (2026).
4. Chen, A., et al.: Generation of surrogates for De-identification of electronic health records. Stud. Health Technol. Inform. **264**, 70–73 (2019)
5. Mir, T.H., et al.: Deidentification and temporal normalization of the electronic health record notes using large language models: the 2023 SREDH/AI-cup competition for Deidentification of sensitive health information. In: International Workshop on Deidentification of Electronic Medical Record Notes. Springer (2024)

6. Radford, A., et al.: Robust speech recognition via large-scale weak supervision. In: International Conference on Machine Learning. PMLR (2023)
7. Jonnagaddala, J., Wong, Z.S.-Y.: Privacy preserving strategies for electronic health records in the era of large language models. npj Digit. Med. **8**(1), 34 (2025)
8. Yunjie Ji, Y., Deng, Y., Li, X.: BELLE: Be Everyone's Large Language Model Engine. GitHub (2023)
9. BYVoid, OpenCC. (2010).
10. OpenNMT, CTranslate2. (2018).
11. Jonnagaddala, J., et al.: The OpenDeID corpus for patient de-identification. Sci. Rep. **11**(1), 19973 (2021)
12. Panchal, O., et al.: Benchmarking Large Language Models for De-identification of Electronic Health Record Notes. (2026).
13. Yang, A., et al., Qwen3 technical report. arXiv preprint https://arxiv.org/abs/2505.09388, (2025).
14. Xu, L., et al.: Parameter-efficient fine-tuning methods for pretrained language models: A critical review and assessment. arXiv preprint https://arxiv.org/abs/2312.12148, (2023).
15. Hu, E.J., et al.: Lora: low-rank adaptation of large language models. ICLR. **1**(2), 3 (2022)
16. Dettmers, T., et al.: Qlora: efficient finetuning of quantized llms. Adv. Neural Inf. Proces. Syst. **36**, 10088–10115 (2023)

A Generative Large Language Model–based Approach for Sensitive Data Identification in Medical Speech

Li Zheng-Hao[1](✉) [iD] and Hong-Jie Dai[1,2,3,4] [iD]

[1] Intelligent System Laboratory, Department of Electrical Engineering, National Kaohsiung University of Science and Technology, Kaohsiung, Taiwan
{f112154147,hjdai}@nkust.edu.tw
[2] Nation Institute of Cancer Research, National Health Research Institutes, Tainan, Taiwan
[3] School of Post-Baccalaureate Medicine, College of Medicine, Kaohsiung Medical University, Kaohsiung, Taiwan
[4] Center for Big Data Research, Kaohsiung Medical University, Kaohsiung, Taiwan

Abstract. This paper presents the methodology and results of our entry (TEAM_7897) in the AI CUP 2025 Spring Season "Medical Speech Sensitive Personal Data Identification" competition. The primary challenge was to accurately extract sensitive personal information and corresponding timestamps from medical dialogue transcripts. To address this, we propose a comprehensive pipeline that reframes the named entity recognition task as a generative problem using a large language model. At the core of the system is the Qwen3-8B model, fine-tuned efficiently via low-rank adaptation to recognize and format entities. A key innovation is a two-step data augmentation strategy designed to mitigate the severe class imbalance in the dataset: first generating novel entity examples, then producing realistic contextual sentences. Automatic speech recognition was performed using *openai/whisper-large-v3*. Notably, the native Whisper model (mixed error rate: 0.152) outperformed its fine-tuned version, and the NER model trained solely on the original dataset surpassed the model trained with augmented data. Analysis revealed that limitations in the quality and diversity of the generated data hindered performance. These findings demonstrate the potential of generative LLMs for complex NER tasks while emphasizing that data quality is critical for effective augmentation pipelines.

Keywords: Named Entity Recognition · Large Language Models · Qwen3 · Whisper · Data Augmentation · Medical Speech Processing · Parameter-efficient Fine-tuning

1 Introduction

Automatic identification of sensitive personal information in unstructured text typically addressed through named entity recognition (NER)—is a critical task for ensuring privacy across domains. In the medical field, doctor–patient conversations contain substantial amounts of sensitive data, including names, dates, identification numbers, and medical record numbers. Accurate and automated redaction of such information is essential for effective anonymization and compliance with privacy regulations.

Recent benchmarking studies have demonstrated that large language models achieve state-of-the-art performance across a wide range of natural language processing tasks, highlighting their effectiveness for complex information extraction problems [1].

Recent work has explored the use of large language models for identifying sensitive entities in clinical documents [2]. Chen et al. [3] propose a method for improving the **de-identification of electronic health records (EHRs)** through the **generation of realistic surrogate values to replace protected health information (PHI)**. Instead of simply removing sensitive identifiers such as names, locations, or dates, their approach replaces them with contextually appropriate synthetic alternatives that preserve the structure and readability of the original clinical text.

However, the task is challenged by the diversity of entity types and their highly imbalanced distribution within datasets. The increasing use of large language models on electronic health records introduces significant privacy risks, making robust de-identification strategies essential for the safe secondary use of clinical data [4]. Many entities appear infrequently, limiting a model's ability to learn their patterns reliably.

To address these issues, we developed a system for the AI CUP 2025 competition [5] that reframes NER as a generative, instruction-following task by leveraging the advanced capabilities of large language models (LLMs).

The primary contributions of this study are as follows:

Generative NER Framework. We employ Qwen3-8B, an instruction-tuned LLM, to directly generate structured entity outputs. This generative formulation naturally handles complex cases such as overlapping or discontinuous entities and can be readily extended to new entity categories.

Innovative Data Augmentation. To mitigate the long-tail distribution of entity types, we introduce a two-step data augmentation strategy. First, the method generates diverse seed entities for low-frequency classes; subsequently, it produces high-quality, contextually coherent sentences incorporating these seeds.

Robust Timestamp Alignment. We develop a flexible alignment algorithm that uses Levenshtein distance–based fuzzy matching to accurately link predicted entity text to timestamped tokens from ASR output, even in the presence of minor transcription errors or intervening words.

This paper presents the proposed methodology, covering the complete pipeline from the initial ASR processing to LLM fine-tuning and the data augmentation strategies designed to enhance model performance.

1.1 Related Work

The NER task has been an active area of research in the medical domain for many years. Conventional approaches have frequently relied on feature-based statistical models, e.g., hidden Markov models, conditional random fields (CRFs), and support vector machines. Note that these methods require extensive feature engineering, relying on handcrafted features, e.g., part-of-speech tags, capitalization, and domain-specific dictionaries (gazetteers). While effective to a degree, these methods frequently struggle to generalize to unseen patterns.

With the emergence of deep learning, recurrent neural networks, particularly long short-term memory (LSTM) and gated recurrent unit networks, have become the standard. Bidirectional LSTM models combined with a CRF layer (BiLSTM-CRF) are a dominant architecture because they can capture contextual information and sequence dependencies effectively. In addition, introducing pretrained language models, e.g., the BERT model and its variants, further revolutionized the field by providing rich, contextualized word embeddings, which improves performance on various NER benchmarks considerably.

The ASR task is the foundation of the proposed pipeline. We utilize the Whisper model [6], which has demonstrated robustness in multilingual settings.

Recently, LLMs have introduced a new paradigm for NER. Instead of treating NER as a token-level classification task, researchers have begun exploring generative formulations. Prior studies [7, 8] have shown that LLMs can reliably extract structured entities through instruction following. This approach, which we adopt here, offers several advantages: it handles complex, nested, or discontinuous entities more naturally than token-based classifiers and supports zero-shot or few-shot learning through prompt modification alone. Building on this trend, the present study applies a state-of-the-art, instruction-tuned LLM (Qwen3-8B) and leverages parameter-efficient fine-tuning (PEFT) techniques to ensure computational efficiency. In addition, our LLM-driven data augmentation strategy directly addresses the longstanding issue of data scarcity in specialized domains such as medicine.

2 Methodology

The proposed multistage pipeline is illustrated in Fig. 1. The pipeline begins with ASR, which is followed by data augmentation and NER model fine-tuning processes. It concludes with an alignment step to produce the final output.

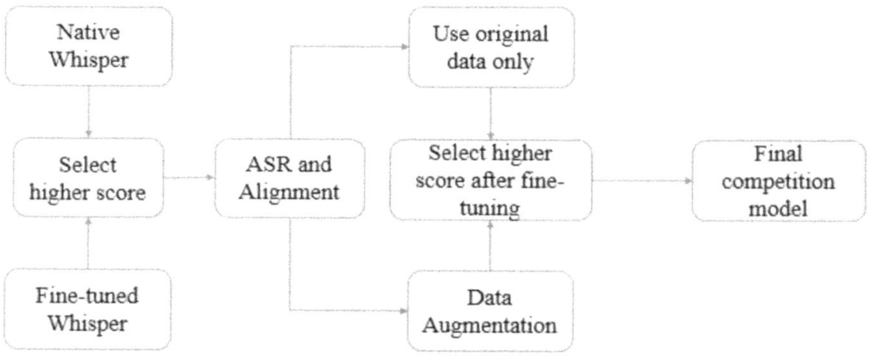

Fig. 1. The overall design flow of our model.

Model Selection Strategy: Figure 1 shows the optimization pipeline; however, it is important to clarify that the flow represents a competitive selection framework. In this study, we did not default to using the fine-tuned or augmented models. Instead, the final system configuration (Native Whisper + Original Data Model) was selected based on the **superior empirical performance on the validation set**, which ensures that our final submission maximizes accuracy, even if it means discarding modifications (fine-tuning/augmentation) that did not yield performance gains in the target domain.

2.1 Dataset

The experiments in this study utilize the **SREDH-AICup SHI speech corpus 2025 corpus**, a gold-standard dataset designed for research on automated de-identification of electronic health records. The corpus contains **2,100 pathology reports collected from 1,833 cancer patients**, with each report averaging roughly 700 tokens. Within these reports, **38,414 protected health information (PHI) entities** have been manually annotated, enabling the development and evaluation of models for identifying sensitive information in clinical text [9]. The dataset was carefully curated through manual annotation and surrogate replacement to ensure that no identifiable patient information remains while preserving realistic clinical context for machine learning research [10].

2.2 System Architecture and Task Formulation

The competition was divided into two main tasks.

Task 1 (ASR). Here, the speech files are transcribed to text using the openai/whisper-large-v3 model. We compared the performance of the native, pretrained Whisper model against a version that was fine-tuned on the competition's data.

Task 2 (NER). Here, sensitive entities are extracted from the transcribed text. Note that this task requires the output to be a specific string format (Type1\tText1##Type2\tText2...) or the string "Null" if no entities are found. We treated this task as a conditional text generation task for an LLM.

The decision to frame NER as a generative task was intentional. Conventional token-classification models typically employ the BIO (Beginning, Inside, Outside) tagging schema to assign labels to individual tokens. In this framework, B- prefixes (e.g., B-PER) mark the first token of an entity, I- prefixes (e.g., I-PER) denote subsequent tokens within the same entity, and O represents tokens outside of any named entity.

While common, these models often struggle with nested entities (e.g., "[Dr. Smith]'s office at [St. Jude Hospital]") and discontinuous entities (e.g., "the patient was prescribed Tylenol … which she took yesterday"). In contrast, a generative model learns to "read" the entire text and "write" a structured summary of the extracted entities, making it inherently more flexible and better suited to complex entity configurations. Moreover, adding new entity types becomes substantially simpler, as it only requires updating the prompt and providing new training examples rather than modifying the model's output architecture.

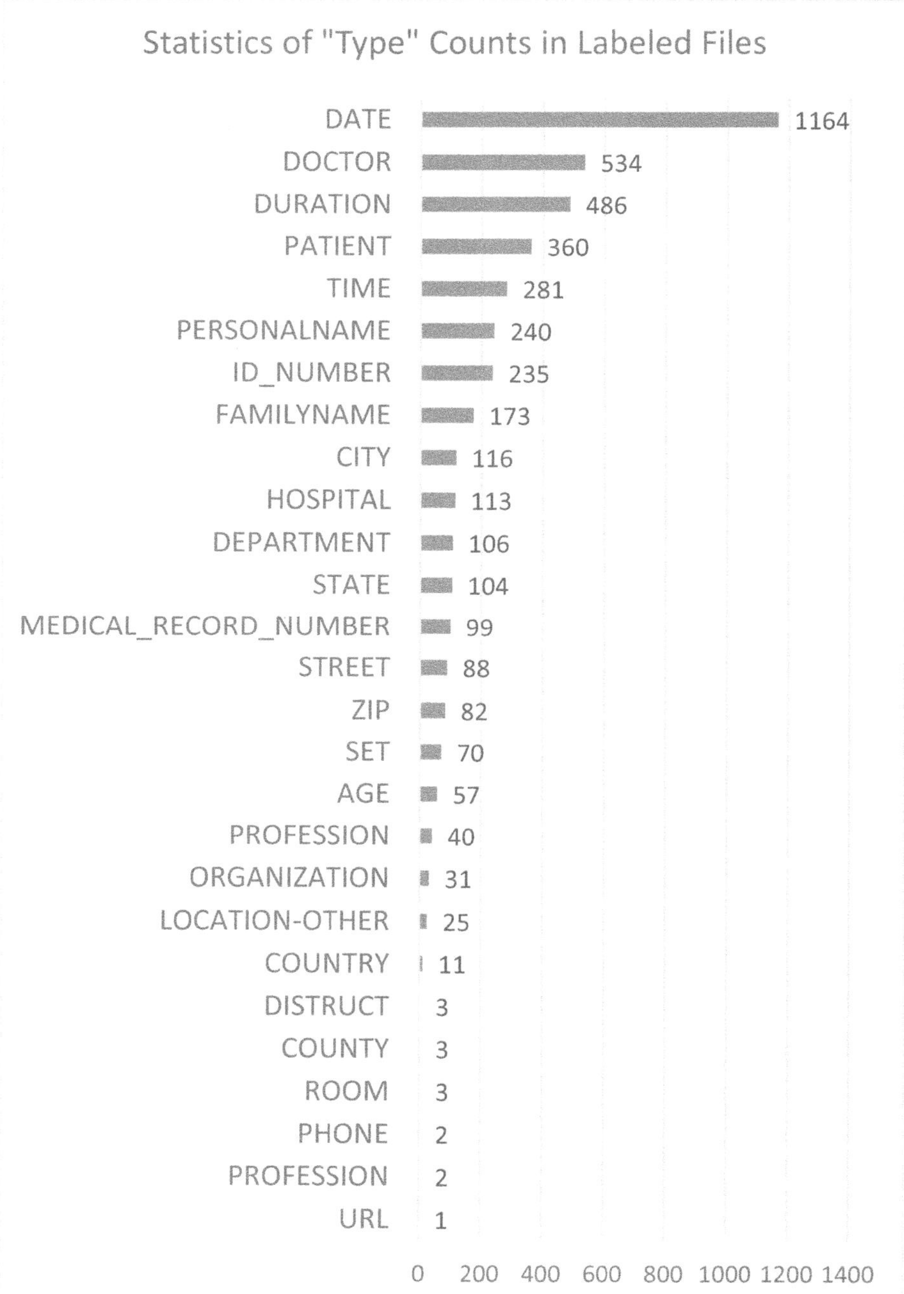

Fig. 2. The frequency distribution of entity types in the annotation file.

2.3 Data Analysis and Preprocessing

In this study, the dataset consisted of audio files, their corresponding transcripts (*task1_answer.txt*), and annotations of sensitive information (*task2_answer.txt*). An initial analysis of the entity distribution revealed a pronounced long-tail pattern (Fig. 2). For instance, the DATE entity appeared 1,164 times, whereas the URL entity appeared only once. This imbalance—where many categories fell below the target threshold of 60 samples—served as the primary motivation for developing our data augmentation strategy.

2.4 Two-Step Data Augmentation

To address the data scarcity issue for low-frequency entity types, we designed a two-step data augmentation process using the Qwen3-32B model (Fig. 3).

Step 1 (Variant Seed Generation). For each entity type with fewer than 60 samples, we prompted the LLM to generate new, diverse entity examples. For example, given the original seed "salon.com" for the URL type, the model would generate new seeds, e.g., "medinfo.org" and "patient-resources.net." This step directly addresses the lack of instance diversity in the original dataset. Here, we employed batch generation and rigorous postprocessing to ensure the uniqueness and validity of the generated seeds.

Step 2 (Contextual Sentence Generation).We then prompted the LLM to create realistic medical-context sentences using the generated seeds. Here, to ensure the style was consistent with the target domain, we provided sentences from the original corpus as style references in the prompt. This "style guide" approach was crucial in terms of ensuring the semantic validity of the generated text, constraining the LLM to produce medically plausible sentences that are similar to the source distribution.

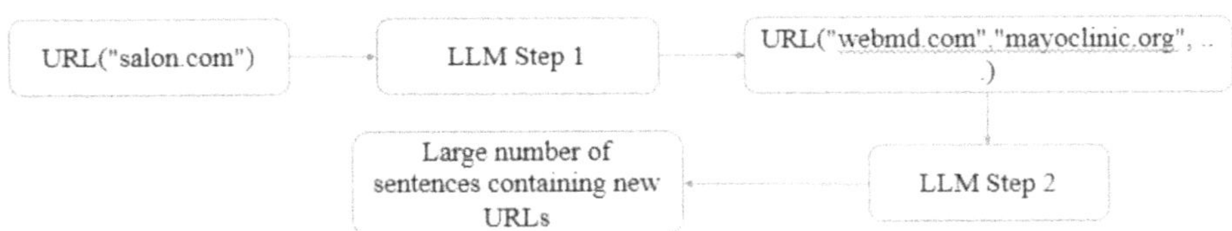

Fig. 3. The data augmentation process, using the URL entity type as an example.

Prompt engineering played a critical role in this process. For Step 1 (Variant Seed Generation), the prompt provided few-shot examples of the target entity type along with strict instructions to produce only a list of new, similar entities and no explanatory text. For Step 2 (Contextual Sentence Generation), the prompt was more elaborate: it included (1) the newly generated seed entity, (2) a randomly selected sentence from the original corpus to serve as a stylistic reference, and (3) a directive to generate a medically relevant sentence that naturally incorporates the seed. To further increase contextual diversity, we cycled through several instruction templates (e.g., "Write a sentence a doctor might say," "Write a sentence that could appear in a patient's medical record").

2.5 NER Model Architecture

In this study, we selected the Qwen3-8B model [11] as the base model for the generative NER task. As an 8-billion parameter instruction-tuned causal language model, the Qwen3-8B model excels at understanding and following complex instructions; thus, it is ideal for our task formulation. To adapt this large model to the target task under computational constraints, we employed PEFT, specifically low-rank adaptation (LoRA) [12]. As shown in Fig. 4, we froze the massive pretrained weights of the Qwen3-8B model (loaded in 4-bit precision via bitsandbytes) and injected trainable low-rank decomposition matrices (rank $r = 16$) into the linear layers. This architecture allows the model to learn task-specific patterns efficiently while keeping the vast majority of parameters fixed.

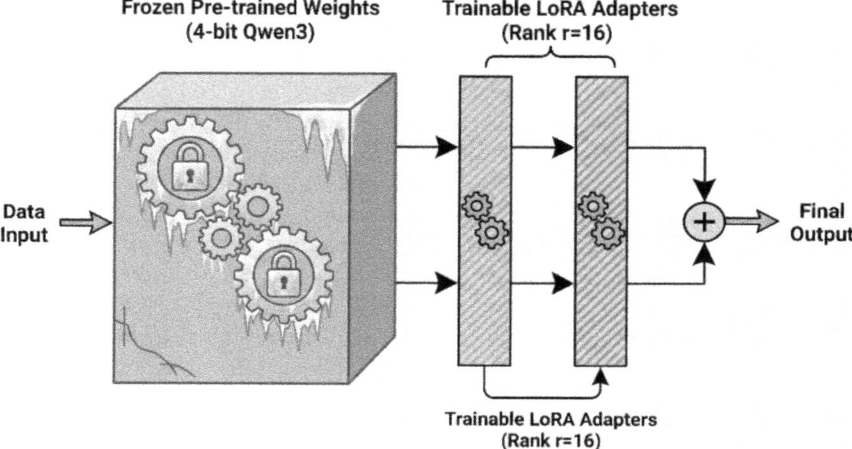

Fig. 4. Schematic illustration of our Parameter-Efficient Fine-Tuning (PEFT) architecture. The pre-trained Qwen3-8B base model (left) is quantized to 4-bit and frozen to minimize memory usage. Trainable Low-Rank Adaptation (LoRA) adapters with a rank of $r = 16$ (right) are injected into the transformer layers to learn task-specific features, and their outputs are summed with the frozen path to produce the final result.

2.6 Timestamp Alignment Algorithm

A key component of the inference pipeline is the alignment of entities predicted by the NER model with the word-level timestamps produced by the ASR system. To achieve this, we developed a flexible alignment algorithm featuring two main capabilities.

Fuzzy Matching. The algorithm uses the Levenshtein distance [13] to compare predicted entity tokens with ASR tokens, allowing for minor spelling discrepancies introduced by ASR errors (e.g., "Francio" vs. "Franco").

Flexible-gap Handling. The algorithm also permits a limited number of unrelated intervening words within a multiword entity, enabling accurate alignment even when the ASR output splits conceptually continuous phrases (e.g., *"last week's"* rendered as *last* [5.07–5.33] and *week's* [5.43–5.69]).

The proposed alignment algorithm operates as follows. First, each predicted entity string is tokenized into individual words. The algorithm then iterates through the ASR's timestamped word list to identify the sequence that provides the best fuzzy match for the entity. A *search_start_index* is maintained to prevent previously matched ASR words from being reused for subsequent entities within the same sentence, thereby ensuring correct handling of repeated text. When evaluating a candidate match for a multiword entity, the algorithm permits up to a predefined number of intervening nonmatching ASR words (*max_intervening_words = 1*). This threshold was selected based on preliminary validation experiments: a value of 0 failed to capture cases where an entity was split in the ASR output (e.g., *"last week's"* → *"last," "week's"*), whereas thresholds of 2 or more produced excessive false positives. The final entity timestamp is derived from the start time of the first matched word and the end time of the last matched word.

3   Training and Implementation Details

3.1   Experimental Setup

All experiments in this study were conducted on a workstation equipped with a single NVIDIA RTX 6000 Ada Generation GPU with 48 GB of VRAM. The software environment was based on Python 3.10. PyTorch served as the core deep learning framework, and several Hugging Face ecosystem libraries were used: *transformers* for model loading, *datasets* for data handling, *accelerate* for streamlined training, and *peft* for the LoRA implementation. The *bitsandbytes* library was also employed to enable model quantization.

3.2   Model Loading and Quantization

To manage the memory footprint of the Qwen3-8B model, we utilized 4-bit quantization via the bitsandbytes library. Here, the model was loaded with the following configuration.

load_in_4bit = True
bnb_4bit_quant_type = "nf4" (NormalFloat 4)
bnb_4bit_compute_dtype = torch.bfloat16
bnb_4bit_use_double_quant = True

These settings reduced the GPU memory requirement from approximately 16 GB to 5 GB, thereby allowing for efficient training.

3.3 LoRA Fine-Tuning

We employed the peft library to implement LoRA with the following configuration.

r = 16 (rank of adaptation matrices)

lora_alpha = 32 (scaling factor)

lora_dropout = 0.05

target_modules: applied to all key linear layers in the Transformer architecture (q_proj, k_proj, v_proj, o_proj, etc.)

This configuration resulted in 43,646,976 trainable parameters out of a total of 8,234,382,336 parameters, representing precisely 0.5301% of the model capacity. This demonstrates the high efficiency of the fine-tuning strategy.

3.4 Training Process

Model training in this study was conducted using the Hugging Face *Trainer*. The NER task was reformulated as a causal language modeling problem in which the model learns to generate the target text conditioned on the input text. We used the AdamW optimizer with a cosine learning rate schedule, a learning rate of $2e-4$, and an effective batch size of 8. Two models were trained: one using only the original dataset and another using a combination of the original and augmented datasets (Table 1).

Table 1. Training Datasets

Models	Total sentences
Model 1 (Original Data)	2,314
Augmented Data Only	403
Model 2 (Combined)	2,717

4 Results

The final performance of our models was evaluated on the private leaderboard, which represents the official competition results calculated using a hidden, unseen test dataset. These results are summarized in Tables 2 and 3.

Table 2. Task 1 Model Performance (mixed error rate, MER)

Model	MER
Native Whisper	0.1523
Fine-tuned Whisper	0.1734

Table 3. Task 2 Model Performance (F1-score)

Model	Precision	Recall	F1-score
Model 1 (Original Data)	0.5258	0.5098	0.5177
Model 2 (Augmented Data)	0.4633	0.5051	0.4733

The best-performing configuration combined the native Whisper-large-v3 model for ASR with the NER model trained solely on the original dataset. Notably, fine-tuning Whisper resulted in a counterintuitive performance decline (MER 0.1734 vs. 0.1523). This degradation is likely due to *catastrophic forgetting*. Although the competition dataset is domain-specific, it is far smaller and less diverse than the corpus used to pretrain Whisper-large-v3. As a result, fine-tuning likely caused the model to overfit to the narrow acoustic characteristics of the training set, reducing the broad generalization capabilities encoded in the pretrained weights.

4.1 Analysis of Data Augmentation Failure

In theory, data augmentation should have improved performance, particularly for low-frequency classes. However, qualitative analysis of the augmented dataset revealed several critical issues, as illustrated in Figs. 5, 6, and 7.

Mixed Languages. The LLM frequently produced sentences containing both English and Chinese, resulting in degraded data quality (Fig. 5).

These issues indicate that, while LLM-based data augmentation is a powerful approach, its effectiveness depends heavily on precise prompt engineering and rigorous validation to ensure the quality, diversity, and correctness of the generated data.

Fig. 5. Example of poor-quality augmented data with mixed Chinese and English.

Lack of Diversity. The generated sentences frequently exhibited very similar syntactic structures, failing to provide the model with sufficiently varied examples (Fig. 6).

```
The patient mentioned researching alternat
The patient mentioned reading about alterna
You can easily schedule your medical appoir
Have you checked out the latest updates on
their policies.
You can read more about this condition and
The patient mentioned they found relief th

The patient mentioned reading an article cr
To schedule your medical appointment or get

I found some information on drguidelines.co
You can find more information about your co
The patient mentioned reading an article at
The patient mentioned they found our clinic
If you need to book an appointment or get a
You can find detailed information about med
You can read more about this condition in a
The patient mentioned they found helpful in
The patient mentioned they found our clinic
You can read more about the new online sche
For more information on medical billing pro
You can read more about this condition and
The patient mentioned accessing additional
The patient was instructed to review their
```

Fig. 6. Example of generated sentences with low diversity in structure.

Incomplete Annotations. A more serious issue arose when the LLM generated sentences containing multiple sensitive entities but was instructed to label only the single "seed" entity. All additional entities in the generated text remained unlabeled, producing noisy training data in which the model implicitly learned to ignore valid entities. This likely reduced model precision (Fig. 7). Notably, precision dropped from 0.5258 (Model 1) to 0.4633 (Model 2), a decline that directly correlates with this annotation noise.

The unlabeled sensitive entities effectively acted as "poisoned" negative samples. During training, the model was penalized for correctly identifying entities that appeared in the text but were absent from the ground truth labels, ultimately pushing it toward overly conservative predictions.

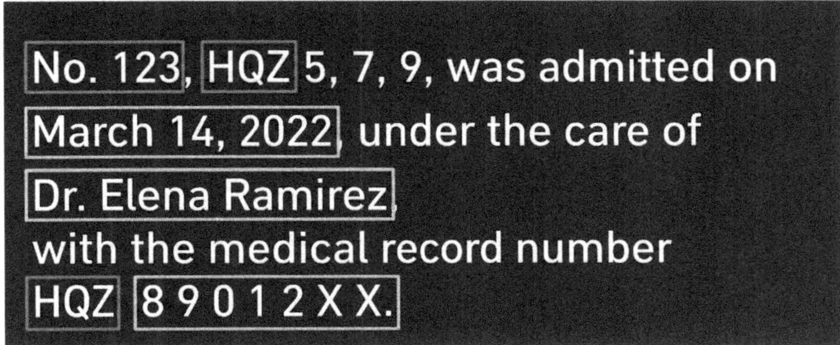

Fig. 7. Example of a generated sentence with an unlabeled sensitive entity, creating noisy data.

These issues highlight that the success of LLM-based data augmentation is highly dependent on meticulous prompt engineering and a robust validation process to ensure the quality, diversity, and correctness of the generated data.

4.2 Error Analysis

Beyond the failure of the augmentation strategy, we performed an error analysis on the predictions of the best-performing model (Model 1). The errors can be broadly categorized as follows.

Boundary Errors. The model correctly identified an entity but failed to capture its precise boundaries. For example, the model may predict "Dr. Smith" rather than the full "Dr. Smith's office" or "last week" rather than "sometime last week." We found that this was one of the most common error types.

Misclassification Errors. The model correctly identified an entity span; however, it assigned it the wrong type, e.g., classifying a hospital name (HOSPITAL) as a generic organization (ORGANIZATION). This type of error occurred most frequently between closely related entity types.

Spurious Predictions. The model predicted an entity that was not present in the ground truth. This occurred frequently with common words or phrases that could be entities in other contexts (e.g., identifying "today" as a DATE when it was not annotated).

Missed Entities. The model completely failed to identify an entity. This error type was overwhelmingly concentrated in the tail-end of the distribution shown in Fig. 2. Here, low-frequency categories, e.g., URL, PHONE, and ID_NUMBER, accounted for most missed entities, which confirms that the model struggled to generalize from sparse examples despite the augmentation attempts.

4.3 Ablation Study: Robustness of Timestamp Alignment

To evaluate the contribution of the proposed flexible timestamp alignment module to the overall system performance, we conducted an ablation study by replacing it with a baseline "strict string-matching" approach. The results, summarized in Table 4, highlight the impact of this specific component on the final output.

1. Effect of Fuzzy Matching. Incorporating Levenshtein distance–based fuzzy matching instead of exact string matching increased the F1-score by 1.42% ($0.4925 \rightarrow 0.5067$). This improvement was mainly due to correctly recovering entities affected by minor ASR spelling errors (e.g., *"Francio"* vs. *"Franco"*).

2. Effect of Flexible Gaps. Allowing *max_intervening_words = 1* significantly improved recall for multiword entities split in the ASR output. Compared to *max_intervening_words = 0*, this flexible-gap strategy contributed an additional 1.1% to the F1-score, raising it to 0.5177.

Table 4. Results of Ablation Study of Timestamp Alignment Strategies (on Validation Set)

Method	Precision	Recall	F1-Score
Baseline (Strict Matching, Gap = 0)	0.5010	0.4845	0.4925
+ Fuzzy Matching Only (Levenshtein)	0.5180	0.4960	0.5067
Proposed Full Method (Fuzzy + Gap = 1)	0.5258	0.5098	0.5177

5   Discussion

5.1   Limitations

This study has several limitations. First, the analysis was restricted to the competition dataset, which, although representative, may not capture the full variability of medical dialogues. Second, our experiments focused on a single LLM architecture (Qwen3-8B); models with different architectures or pretraining objectives may perform differently. Third, the data augmentation process was fully automated. Incorporating a human-in-the-loop to validate or correct generated data could likely improve results, but at a higher cost. Finally, our study considered only English and Traditional Chinese medical dialogues, limiting the direct generalizability of the findings to other languages without additional adaptation.

Advanced Prompting Techniques. More sophisticated prompting strategies, e.g., chain-of-thought or self-correction strategies should be investigated. For example, the model could be prompted to first "think" about which entities might be in a sentence prior to generating the final structured output, potentially improving accuracy. Refined Data Augmentation with Validation. The data augmentation pipeline should be enhanced with a validation step. This could involve using a separate, smaller model to score the quality of the generated sentences or, more robustly, incorporating a human-in-the-loop system where human annotators quickly review and approve or reject the augmented samples.

Investigating Different Model Architectures. Testing other larger and smaller LLMs could provide insights into the tradeoffs between model size, performance, and computational cost for the target task. Multitask Learning. The model could be fine-tuned on a combination of related tasks, e.g., NER and relation extraction, to encourage it to learn more robust and generalizable representations of the text.

6 Conclusion

In this study, we developed a complete NER pipeline leveraging a generative LLM, reframing entity extraction as an instruction-following task and demonstrating the flexibility of modern LLMs. Although our two-step data augmentation strategy did not deliver the expected improvements due to quality control issues, it provided valuable insights into the challenges of synthetic data generation and the importance of data integrity in training generative models.

Future work should focus on enhancing the data augmentation pipeline through more sophisticated prompt engineering for seed and sentence generation, as well as implementing a "validator" model to assess and filter augmented data for quality and accuracy before training.

Our findings underscore a key lesson: in the era of LLMs, data quality often outweighs data quantity. A smaller, cleaner dataset proved more effective than a larger, noisier one. While generative NER remains a promising approach, its success critically depends on the quality of the data and the precision of the instructions used in fine-tuning.

Acknowledgments. This work was supported by the Ministry of Education and the National Science and Technology Council under grant *NSTC112-2221-E-992-056-MY3*.

Disclosure of Interests. The authors declare that they have no competing interests relevant to the content of this article.

References

1. Panchal, O., et al., Benchmarking Large Language Models for De-Identification of Electronic Health Record Notes. (2026).
2. Dai, H.-J., et al.: Leveraging large language models for the deidentification and temporal normalization of sensitive health information in electronic health records. npj Digit. Med. **8**(1), 517 (2026)
3. Chen, A., et al.: Generation of surrogates for De-identification of electronic health records. Stud. Health Technol. Inform. **264**, 70–73 (2019)
4. Jonnagaddala, J., Wong, Z.S.-Y.: Privacy preserving strategies for electronic health records in the era of large language models. npj Digital Medicine. **8**(1), 34 (2025)
5. Dai, H.-J., et al., *Leveraging State-of-the-Art LLMs for the De-identification of Sensitive Health Information in Clinical Speech.* medRxiv, : p. 2026.04.13.26349911 (2026).
6. Radford, A., et al. *Robust speech recognition via large-scale weak supervision.* in *International conference on machine learning.* PMLR (2023).
7. Yan, H., et al.: *A unified generative framework for various NER subtasks.* in *Proceedings of the 59th Annual Meeting of the Association for Computational Linguistics and the 11th International Joint Conference on Natural Language Processing (Volume 1: Long Papers).* (2021).
8. Wang, S., et al. *Gpt-ner: Named entity recognition via large language models.* in *Findings of the association for computational linguistics: NAACL 2025.* (2025).
9. Jonnagaddala, J., et al.: The OpenDeID corpus for patient de-identification. Sci. Rep. **11**(1), 19973 (2021)
10. Dai, H.J., et al.: A Clinical Speech Corpus with Temporally Aligned Sensitive Health Information (2026). https://www.medrxiv.org/content/10.64898/2026.03.31.26349906v2

11. Yang, A., et al., *Qwen3 technical report.* arXiv preprint https://arxiv.org/abs/2505.09388, (2025).
12. Hu, E.J., et al.: Lora: low-rank adaptation of large language models. Iclr. **1**(2), 3 (2022)
13. Levenshtein, V.I.: Binary codes capable of correcting deletions, insertions, and reversals. In: Soviet Physics Doklady. Soviet Union (1966)

Author Index

GPSR Compliance
The European Union's (EU) General Product Safety Regulation (GPSR) is a set
of rules that requires consumer products to be safe and our obligations to
ensure this.

If you have any concerns about our products, you can contact us on

ProductSafety@springernature.com

In case Publisher is established outside the EU, the EU authorized
representative is:

Springer Nature Customer Service Center GmbH
Europaplatz 3
69115 Heidelberg, Germany